BURIED ALIVE FOR CHRIST

And Other Missionary Stories

BURIED ALIVE FOR CHRIST
And Other Missionary Stories

V. BEN KENDRICK

Foreword by Allan E. Lewis
Illustrations by Steven Rockwell

REGULAR BAPTIST PRESS
1300 North Meacham Road
Post Office Box 95500
Schaumburg, Illinois 60195

These stories are written from the materials gathered by the author throughout his twenty years of missionary service. In many cases the names have been changed.

Library of Congress Cataloging in Publication Data

Kendrick, V. Ben.
    Buried alive for Christ and other missionary stories.

    1. Missionary stories. I. Title.
BV2087.K44   266'.0096   78-14984
ISBN 0-87227-061-0

It is with deep appreciation that I dedicate this book to my wife, Nina, who encouraged me to write. I also want to take this opportunity to acknowledge the help of Bernice Inman, Sallie McElwain and Joyce Frcho for their work in typing and proofreading.

Contents

Part III: Our Prayer-Answering God

Part IV: The Power of the Word

Part V: Those Precious Jewels

Introduction

AS I READ THE STORIES contained in this volume, I could not help but realize anew how providentially God works in all things pertaining to the proclamation of the gospel to the unregenerate heart. As you read, you will rejoice in the way the Spirit of God prepares those hearts for the reception of His Word. And you will be caused to give thanks for the servants of God who accept the challenge of proclaiming that Word.

In going forth with weeping, bearing precious seed, V. Ben Kendrick laid by in store a vast reservoir of knowledge and experience concerning the lives and customs of the people of Africa. Out of those years of service comes this compilation of stories to form Mr. Kendrick's first book. His insights into the mind and heart of his characters make these accounts come to life for the reader. His lucid style makes for easy reading and understanding.

These chapters first came to my attention when they were submitted separately, over many months' time, as stories for our *Challenge, Certainty* and *Conquest* publications. Though all but a few have been published in that form, I welcome their use in this book.

It is my prayer that through these pages many shall sense the need to pray more fervently for missionaries, give more generously to missions, and yield their lives completely to the Lord for His use on the fields that are white unto harvest.

Darrell R. Bice, Editor
Regular Baptist Press
Schaumburg, Illinois

cutting his lip and causing his nose to bleed.

"The Lord loves you," whispered Andrew, "and wants to give you eternal life."

"Shut up, you fool!" called the leader of the soldiers. "Bow down in the name of the president."

"I can't," said Andrew. "Only the living God of Heaven is my God and deserves my worship."

"You dog! We'll make you drink your own blood out of your hands," cried the leader.

"I belong to the Lord," said Andrew softly.

A heavy boot landed in the middle of his back, nearly doubling him backwards and sending him sprawling once again into the dirt. Kick after kick followed, and Andrew's body was racked with pain. His face, back and stomach were kicked and kicked again. When he had almost reached unconsciousness, Andrew felt a heavy blow on his legs and heard the snap of bones. Someone had located a long iron bar and had swung it down across Andrew's shins.

"Please, Lord, take me Home quickly. Help me to glorify You even in death," Andrew prayed in his heart.

Andrew must have fainted. The next thing he vaguely knew, he was being held in a sitting position and water was being thrown into his face. "Get a shovel and a pick. Let's bury the animal alive," someone called out. All alone among so many enemies, Andrew, half-conscious, prayed for them and, at the same time, asked God to take him Home to be with Him.

"Here, dig, you fool," said one of the soldiers, forcing the pick into Andrew's hands. "Dig, I said! Dig! Dig!" came the command, accompanied by cursing and by heavy blows of the rifle butt.

Andrew tried to strike the ground with the pick, but his strength was gone and his broken legs pained him unbearably. He fainted but was revived again, only to see that he was lying at the side of a hole. "Now, will you deny your faith, you missionary-follower?" asked one of the soldiers. "Take a look at your doom and still refuse, if you can."

Andrew began to sing softly through his puffed lips, "Face to face with Christ, my Savior, Face to face, what will it be? When with rapture I behold Him, Jesus Christ who died for me."

"That's enough of that nonsense. Stuff his mouth with dirt," yelled the commanding officer. "Our job is to make him deny his faith and give in to our president's decree, or else to kill him." A

19

face came close to Andrew's, and a voice clearly said, "Look, my brother, you are one of us. Just say that you will support our government, and that you reject all of that rubbish that you have heard from the missionaries and read in that book. Tell us, and you will live!"

Andrew looked at him through swollen eyelids. He could hardly make out the blurred object before him. Through his fogged and clouded thinking came the words of the apostle Paul in Philippians 1:20: "Christ shall be magnified in my body, whether it be by life, or by death." Again and again the words echoed in Andrew's mind, "Christ shall be magnified . . . magnified . . . magnified . . . life . . . death . . . death . . . death." And with this, Andrew slipped again into unconsciousness.

The next moments were those which would frighten anyone, but for Andrew it was the reality of the wonderful truth that to be absent from his body is to be present with the Lord. His body filled with pain and his mind sluggishly returning to what was actually taking place, he landed with a thud in the bottom of the hastily dug grave. "Magnify . . . death . . . Jesus . . . life . . . death . . . magnify . . . Heaven . . . Jesus," kept coming to mind.

"Pull him up. Don't cover him completely," ordered the commanding leader. "Others must see and be reminded that they cannot disobey and live to tell of it." Two soldiers reached down and took hold of one of Andrew's broken legs.

Andrew was slipping rapidly beyond the point of feeling pain. A rope was tied around his ankle, pulling him off the bottom of the grave and leaving him suspended, head down, with one leg above the level of the ground. The sharp command came from the rough-looking officer whose bloodshot eyes were fastened on Andrew's sagging and helpless body: "Cover the criminal."

The dirt was piled high around Andrew's still form. "Heaven . . . Jesus . . . Jesus . . . home . . . death . . . Jesus . . . magnify," flashed into the mind of this dying servant. Finally the dirt reached and passed the head of Andrew. With a great, heaving sigh he left his earthly body and entered into the presence of his beloved Lord. The grave was quickly filled. Another savage atrocity had been committed. A swing from the shovel struck the dangling, broken limb, as the soldiers headed back to their truck to continue their search for other believers.

As they walked through the village, one of the soldiers set fire to Andrew's hut and to several others which had been reported to be the homes of believers. Laughter and cursing filled the air. The smell of liquor was everywhere. They climbed into their truck and headed for the next village, leaving behind burning houses and a crude grave containing the body of one of God's chosen servants. The body, buried upside down with one broken leg sticking out of the top of the grave, was to serve as a grim reminder of the cost a believer might pay who takes a stand for God and His holy Word.

2

The Graveside Conversion

DAVID CUPPED HIS HAND to his ear and listened to the drone of a motor in the distance. "Is that a truck I hear, Joseph?" he asked his younger brother who was standing beside him.

Joseph listened a moment. "I think so. It sounds as if it's coming from the village of Yanga, where Paul and Andrew live."

The two brothers, David and Joseph Wanguy, began walking in the direction of the village. They had been traveling for five days through the dense forest to reach their two teenage relatives.

"It sure will be good to see our cousins again," said Joseph as he quickened his pace.

It seemed like ages ago that their Aunt Marie had stopped overnight at their parents' house on her way to the Central African Empire. David's and Joseph's hearts were deeply stirred as she had told of the atrocities committed against the Christians by the government soldiers. She had spoken of the dangers facing her two sons because of their faith in Christ and their love to teach God's Word. While they listened to Aunt Marie, the two brothers decided to try to reach Paul and Andrew.

As they walked along, each seemed to sense what the other was thinking. "I hope the fellows will return with us, David," said Joseph as he tripped over a vine hidden by some leaves.

David stopped in his tracks, staring ahead. "Joseph," he asked, "does that look like smoke?" The younger brother shaded his eyes from the morning sun which penetrated through the trees above them.

"Yes, that's smoke. I'm afraid the village has been burned."

Without speaking another word to each other, the two men carefully made their way to the edge of the forest to view the smoldering village.

"Their house is gone!" David whispered to his brother. "It's that one over there by the road." The two stood in silence behind a bush and carefully scanned the village.

"I don't see any of the villagers," said Joseph. "I wonder if. . . ." Joseph stopped talking and stared at something by the edge of the road.

"What is it, Joseph?" asked David. "What do you see?"

Joseph pointed to something sticking out of the ground, and said, "It's a leg! Someone has been buried upside down!"

David patted his younger brother on the back. "Come on, Joseph. Follow me." The two men stepped out into the village and headed for the grave.

They hadn't taken more than ten steps when they both stopped abruptly. "I hear a motor," whispered David. "I think we should return to the forest and hide."

The sound of the motor became louder, causing the men to run for cover. No sooner had they entered the forest then a government truck came into view down the road.

"Whew!" said David, wiping his brow. "We just made it."

The two young men crouched low in the grass and pulled some brush over them.

"If we're found, David, we'll be killed," said Joseph in a shaky voice.

"Shhh," warned David, holding his hand up to his mouth. "Don't talk. We must be perfectly still."

The truck stopped in the village and several drunken soldiers jumped to the ground. "Look at that fool's leg sticking out of the ground," laughed one of the soldiers.

"We sure took care of him," called another.

"That should teach those Jesus-lovers in this village to support the president's cultural revolution," said still another. "I wonder what it feels like to be buried alive. He sure was a tough one."

One of the men walked over to the grave and kicked the broken, dangling leg. "You traitor," he snarled. "You deserved all that you got." As he walked away, he turned and spit on the grave.

David and Joseph stooped motionless, watching every move

of the men. Both brothers felt sick in their stomachs because of what they saw.

"Come on," called the driver as he looked out the cab window. "I want to get to that next village where I saw that bicycle."

David and Joseph didn't move until the truck was out of sight. "I can't believe that our own people can be so cruel," mumbled David. "They act more like animals than people. Let's go, Joseph."

Once again they left the safety of the forest and stepped out into the village clearing.

"My sons, my sons," called a feeble voice from the tall grass. David and Joseph stopped to see where the voice was coming from. They were surprised to see an old woman step out of the grass and walk toward them.

"Hello, Mama." David shook her hand. "We're looking for Paul and Andrew Wanguy. Have you seen them?"

The old woman bowed her head and began to cry. "They killed them," she sobbed. "They killed Paul yesterday. Today they came back and killed Andrew."

She turned her tearstained face toward the nearby grave. "That's Andrew's body over there." The old woman buried her face in her hands and wept. Both men stood silently beside her.

"Yesterday when they came, they took Paul and beat him with clubs. Then they dragged him into the forest and shot him." As she spoke, David and Joseph could see the agony on her face. She told how the soldiers had come back that morning and had beaten Andrew. "They tried to make him dig his own grave. I'll never forget the terrible sound of his bones breaking when they hit him with an iron bar." Again she stopped to cry.

"You see," she went on, "those two boys were like my own sons. It was their mother who told me about Jesus. I loved those boys." She cried as she spoke.

"Mama," said David with tears running down his face, "we're the boys' cousins. We're their family. We loved them too."

"I'm so glad to see you, but you must go. They'll kill you too."

"We'll go, Mama," said David; "but first we'll bury Andrew's body."

"You'll find a shovel in there," said the old woman, pointing to a nearby hut.

Joseph began to shovel the dirt from around the body of his cousin. It seemed like hours before they were through burying Andrew's body. As the last shovelful of dirt was thrown on the grave, a voice called out from the forest. David looked up to see a young man enter the village.

"Hello there," called David. "Can we help you?"

Before the young man could answer, the old woman spoke. "He was a friend of your cousins. He isn't a Christian even though Paul and Andrew spoke to him many times about Jesus."

The young African stood and listened as she spoke.

"Tega," she continued, "why don't you receive Jesus as your Savior as Paul and Andrew asked you to do? These two men are their cousins, and they know Jesus as their Savior."

The young man stared at the ground.

"That's right, Tega," added Joseph. "Jesus loved you so much that He died to pay the penalty for your sin."

Without saying a word, the teenage boy looked at the fresh grave of his best friend. He thought of the many times Paul and Andrew had witnessed to him about Christ. Tega dropped to his knees. "I'll accept Him," he cried. "I want Him to be my Savior."

There beside the grave of his boyhood friend, Tega opened his heart and received Christ as his Savior. The old woman knelt on one side while David and Joseph knelt on the other side.

"Thank You, Lord," prayed David as the four of them knelt in the half-destroyed village. "Thank You for Paul and Andrew, who even in their death were used by You to bring Tega to Jesus."

The old woman reached over and held Tega's hand. "Yes, thank You, Lord," she prayed.

3

The Escape

THE OLD AFRICAN WOMAN stood in the doorway of her small hut. "I can't believe this is the village where I've lived most of my life." Her tears dropped into the dust at her feet as she viewed the terrible destruction of the soldiers the day before. The government-enforced cultural revolution had brought a reign of terror to the country's Christian population. Many had already died, while others were fleeing for their lives.

"Just look at all those burned houses," she whispered, more to herself than to the three young men standing beside her. "Pastor Luke was shot; Paul was shot; and now Andrew has been buried alive." She hid her face in her hands and sobbed until her frail body seemed as though it would shake apart.

"You boys must return to your village. You must leave quickly. Don't go by way of the road because if the soldiers catch you, they'll kill you too."

"But Mama," said Tega, "what about you? We can't go and leave you."

"Tega, you are still young. You have a whole life ahead of you. Don't risk losing it by staying around here."

She then turned to the nearby grave where Andrew's body lay buried. "Andrew and Paul were just like you men. They loved God and wanted so much to serve Him. After Pastor Luke was shot, the two boys took over the classes and taught the Word of God to us."

The old woman stopped talking for a moment to fight back the tears. Then she continued, "Two days ago the soldiers came back and took Paul into the woods and shot him. I looked for his body but couldn't find it. I'm sure they threw it into the river for the crocodiles." She wiped her eyes with an old rag.

"Yesterday they returned again. I'll never forget what they did to Andrew. He was such a brave boy. I'm sure he was dead even before they threw the last shovel of dirt on the grave. It was right after they drove away that you two boys came out of the forest looking for your cousins."

"We'll carry you, Mama, if you'll come with us," pleaded Joseph.

"No, you boys go on. I haven't many more days to live; so I might as well stay right here. Besides, I don't think they'll harm an old woman." Sadly she looked about her at the destroyed village.

"Now, you must get on your way," she continued, motioning to the forest. "I don't think I could stand it if they caught any of you."

David put out his hand. "Good-bye, Mama. Thank you for putting us up last night and for feeding us. The manioc and corn which you've given us should last the five days that we'll be in the forest."

Joseph and Tega shook her hand as well.

"Tega," she said, "I'm so happy that you accepted Jesus as your Savior yesterday beside Andrew's grave. You are in good company with these two boys. Stay close to them just like you did with Andrew and Paul."

"I will, Mama," said the young teenage boy. "And Mama," he continued, "if you change your mind and want to come on later to the boys' village, send word to us. We'll come and get you."

The three young men prayed with her and then disappeared into the forest.

"I really don't want to leave her," said David, "but I don't want to force her to come either."

"Who knows," added Joseph, "maybe the Lord has a special job for her to do at Yanga."

That night the three young men found cover in some heavy elephant grass beside a stream. As best they could figure, they were about three miles from the main road. Tega left shortly before dark to look for some wild fruit. He hadn't returned.

"I'm getting a bit worried about him, Joseph," said David to his younger brother.

Joseph looked off into the darkness. "I doubt if he could find us at this time of night. Do you think one of us should go look for him, David?"

"No, not yet. Let's wait a little longer. He knows the forest well, and I don't think that he'll get lost," answered David.

"David!" Joseph whispered; "I hear voices. They're heading this way."

The voices became louder. David finally recognized one of the voices to be that of Tega.

"They're in here, Bata," said Tega as he led the way into the hideout.

"David! Joseph!" called Tega in a low voice; "I want you to meet Bata. He's one of the soldiers who witnessed the deaths of your cousins, Andrew and Paul."

The khaki-colored uniform gave the two young men a strange feeling.

"Hello, David. Hello, Joseph," said the young soldier, extending his hand for the usual handshake.

"Hello, Bata," said the boys together, wondering why Tega brought a government soldier with him to their hiding place.

"I know you two are filled with questions," said Tega; "so I'll tell you about Bata and why I've brought him with me." Tega hesitated and then continued, "Better yet, Bata, why don't you tell them your story?"

There was a moment of silence as though Bata was looking for a good place to begin. "I'm a Christian," Bata began. "In fact, I accepted Jesus as my Savior one day in my village when Pastor Luke came to tell us about God's Word. I then became a close friend of Pastor Luke and also of your cousins, Andrew and Paul. This was before I went to the big city to join the army." Bata paused a moment. The three young men sat in silence.

"It was while I was in the city that I got out of fellowship with the Lord. I began drinking and gambling. I was also very unhappy and under deep conviction. When the cultural revolution started and the Christians began to be persecuted, I didn't know what to do. If I told anyone that I was a Christian, I probably would have been asked to deny my faith in Christ or die. I kept silent."

"But what about your taking part in the persecutions?" asked David.

"Well, David," answered Bata, "I never took part in any of the persecutions. I knew they were wrong, and even though I

28

was out of fellowship with the Lord, I never set fire to one house or burned one garden. In fact, I never laid a hand on any Christian or took part in any shootings. When they killed Pastor Luke and then Paul and Andrew, it was almost more than I could bear. I hid my face so they wouldn't recognize me." Bata stopped to catch his breath. He felt a lump in his throat and a heaviness in his chest.

"When I saw the soldiers kill those men, I knew that something had to be done. I guess I couldn't hide my feelings any longer because several of them accused me this afternoon of being a traitor. The turning point came when the leader asked if I was a Jesus-lover."

Bata bowed his head and began to weep. "I couldn't deny my Lord any longer. I couldn't go on pretending that I was one of them. When I told them that I was a Christian, I was asked to choose between obeying the cultural revolution decree or die with the disobedient Christians. I chose to die."

"Then what happened?" asked David.

"Well, first of all, they beat me until I was nearly unconscious. Then they decided to take me into the woods and shoot me. While we were walking along, the soldier who was guarding me began whispering to me. He told me that he too was a Christian and didn't want to shoot me. He said that he wished he could make the same decision I had made but was afraid for his life."

"Where were the other soldiers?" questioned Joseph.

"They were walking a little distance behind us, talking among themselves how they were going to torture me before shooting me," answered Bata. "My guard told me that when we came to the first heavy undergrowth, I should make a break for freedom. He said that he would shoot in the opposite direction and try to divert the soldiers."

"I thought I heard a gun," Joseph remarked.

David smiled and looked at Bata. "Go on, Bata."

"The guard's plan worked. He fired his rifle in the other direction, and the soldiers all took off, looking for me."

"But where did you find Tega?" asked Joseph.

"I found him up a tree picking fruit," Bata answered. "He was surprised and scared when he saw me, but I told him not to be afraid. I figured he was a Christian or he would not have been hiding in the forest. When I told him that I was running away from the soldiers, he practically jumped out of the tree and hugged me."

29

David and Joseph looked at Tega in the light of their little fire and could see a big grin on his face.

"Praise the Lord you're here with us, Bata," said David.

"Thank you, David," responded Bata, who seemed to be over his nervousness. "I hope you fellows don't mind if I make your group a foursome."

That night after they ate, the four men quietly sang a hymn and then had prayer together. As they sat around the red coals, Tega seemed to voice the feelings of all their hearts. "Thank You, Lord," he whispered, "for these good friends. Help us to stand for Christ no matter what we have to go through to do it."

"Amen," echoed his three companions.

5

'He Shall Direct Thy Paths'

THROUGH THE DENSE BRUSH which surrounded them, David saw the red glow in the eastern sky which meant the beginning of another day. He looked at his sleeping brother, Joseph, in the semidarkness. "Joseph," he whispered, "wake up. We've got to be on our way."

Joseph stirred and opened his eyes. "I must have really been worn out. I don't think I moved all night long."

The conversation between the two brothers awakened their companions, Tega and Bata. Joseph had forgotten that Bata had joined the trio the night before. He turned to have a good look at the fugitive government soldier, who had escaped from his fellow soldiers after they found out he was a Christian.

"I'm still here," said Bata, as though he had read Joseph's thoughts. "I don't plan to go anywhere except with you fellows."

David thought of the four of them hiding there in the jungle and the strange happenings that had brought them together. For a moment his mind flashed back to the grave of his cousin, Andrew, who was buried alive because of his faith in Christ. There Tega had accepted Christ as his Savior. The fleeing soldier, Bata, had found Tega in the forest, gathering wild fruit for their evening meal. "I know God has a purpose and plan for all of this," said David to himself.

After washing in a nearby stream, the four young men sat around a small fire for their breakfast of roasted manioc and jungle fruit. They had prayed together and started out for David and Joseph's village, which was three more days of walking.

The dry season made it much easier for the men to travel because much of the grass and undergrowth was burned off. They tried to keep as deep in the forest as possible so they would not be detected by the government soldiers. Because of their refusal to go along with the government supported cultural revolution, they were labeled criminals and prime targets.

It was during the third day of their long walk when it happened. The men were making their way down the side of a bank to cross a small, dry, streambed when Joseph called out. "Oh, no," he said as he reached down and grabbed his right leg. "I've been bitten by a mamba snake."

The other three men rushed to his side as the dangerous monster reared its head to strike at Bata.

"Look out, Bata," called Tega, who was close by his side.

Joseph saw the snake about to strike his friend and, even though he was in great pain, swung his arm and knocked the mamba to the ground. David then caught the snake across its neck with his walking stick, breaking its back. Bata quickly finished it by cutting off its head.

Within a minute, David had made a tourniquet of his shirt sleeve and fastened it just above his brother's knee.

"Hold on, Joseph," said Tega as he took his knife and cut deep into the fang marks. He hoped that he could flush out the venom with the flow of blood. The men worked quickly and expertly on their companion.

"I'm cold, David," whispered Joseph to his older brother, who immediately covered him with his shirt. Tega and Bata took off their shirts, too, and laid them over their suffering friend.

"I'm not going to make it, David," said Joseph as the tears welled in his eyes. "The Lord is going to take me Home."

"Don't try to talk, Joseph," said David, wiping the perspiration from his brother's face. He fought hard to keep back the tears. "Father," he prayed in his heart, "if it's Your will, spare my brother's life."

After a short period of time, Joseph cried out in pain while reaching out his arms. "I can't see you."

David moved close to Joseph. "I'm right here, Joseph. I'm not going to leave you," he whispered, patting his brother on the shoulder.

The three men knew that Joseph was dying. Already his sight was gone.

"Sarah," called Joseph, "I'm home. Where are you?"

7

For Culture or for Christ

I.

PHILIP LOOKED UP from his kneeling position in the peanut garden. He had been working nearly two hours, and the sight of strangers approaching the village spelled a short relief.

"Hey there," called the lead man, "where is Pastor Paul?"

A cold chill ran through Philip's body when he noticed that the men were national security police. They were usually sent out on only very important matters.

"My father's over behind the house. He and my mother are planting sweet potatoes," answered Philip with fear in his voice.

The four uniformed men walked quickly to the house and disappeared around the corner. Paul and Elizabeth were just putting in the last of the potatoes. Elizabeth spotted the policemen as soon as they came around the corner of the house.

"They're coming for you now, Paul," she said in a low whisper. "It's just as I saw it in my dream."

"What do you mean, Elizabeth?" asked the tall, gray-haired pastor.

"I didn't tell you, Paul, but two nights ago I had a dream that the police came and took you away. They charged you with trying to undermine the new government decree enforcing the initiation rites."

"But why didn't you tell me, Elizabeth, if those thoughts have been bothering you?"

"I just couldn't, Paul. I didn't want to burden you any more than you are now. You're already carrying a heavy responsibility representing the fifty Baptist churches in their protest against the initiation rites."

Paul stood up as the men approached. "Hello there! Can I do something for you?"

"Are you Pastor Paul?" asked one of the policemen.

"Yes, I am," answered Paul, offering his hand for the usual handshake.

"Forget the handshake, Pastor," spoke the leader in a stern voice. "Come with us."

Before Paul realized what had happened, he was whisked off toward the waiting jeep. Elizabeth and Philip followed close by, begging the policemen to release their loved one. The men pushed Paul into the waiting vehicle and sped off toward town.

"I knew they would take him," cried Elizabeth as she walked back to the house with her son. "I don't know how many times I've dreamed about this very thing. In fact, just two nights ago I saw them come and take him. I woke up screaming for them to let him go. Now it has really happened. Your father has been arrested like a criminal, Philip!"

As the jeep pulled up to the police station, Paul saw that a number of other pastors were there. The vehicle came to a stop, and a foot landed squarely in the middle of Paul's back. "Get out, old man. Get out or I'll kick you out."

Paul was pulled from the jeep and immediately his hands were jerked behind his back. The clicking of the handcuffs told him that he was a prisoner and totally at their mercy.

"OK," yelled one of the commanding officers; "bring the whole lot in here. I'll talk some sense into their thick heads."

Paul quickly counted twelve other pastors. All were handcuffed, and several revealed cuts and bruises on their faces and arms. They were told to sit on the concrete floor of the dimly lighted room. The commanding officer held a bottle of beer in his hand as he spoke.

"Now you men are supposed to represent God, and I don't have to tell you that God expects obedience from all of us." He took a long drink from the brown-colored bottle and then continued. "Our president has issued a decree that every citizen must honor him by supporting the cultural revolution. This means in every way. To show you that we mean business, we are posting soldiers at all of your churches. They are closed as of this moment. Do you understand? There will be no more church services!"

The statement from the half-drunk officer struck grief into the hearts of the pastors. They turned to look at Paul, their eighty-year-old spiritual leader.

"Sir," said Paul, "I would like your permission to say something in behalf of my brothers."

"All right, you have my permission, but hurry it up!"

"I just want to say that we were born and grew up here. This is our native land. We have had freedom to worship our God for many years. Our government has guaranteed that freedom to us."

"You fool!" cried the officer as he kicked Paul. "You mean you *had* freedom. As of now, your freedom is over. Before you are released, every one of you will bow down in the name of our president and promise to support his cultural revolution."

"No! No!" came the response from several of the pastors.

"You're wrong, Sir," said Paul. "We'll never bow down in the name of a man, even if he is our president."

"You idiot!" shouted the crazed officer as he brought the bottle of beer crashing down on Paul's head. Pieces of glass flew into the group of men. "I'll make you eat those words."

Paul felt blood trickle down the side of his face. He lost consciousness as a heavy boot caught him hard under the chin, sending him sprawling among his co-workers.

About four o'clock the next morning, the men were herded into the back of an army truck and taken across town to the presidential palace. As they made their way into the heavily guarded mansion, they were surprised to find the president waiting for them.

"Hello, my brothers," he greeted them, with a big smile spread across his face. "I'm sorry for what happened to you last night. That was all a terrible mistake, and I apologize. I want you to join me for breakfast, and then you can all go home to your families and do the work of God in your churches."

The handcuffs were removed from each of the men, and they were led to a long table in a nearby room. Never had they seen so much food.

"Sit down, my brothers," said the president as he took his place at the head of the huge table. "Pastor Paul, as the spiritual father of all of us, why don't you thank God for our food?"

The surprised group of pastors bowed their heads as Paul prayed. "Thank You, Father, for Your watchcare over us during the night. Be with our families while we are absent from them. And, Lord, I pray, too, that You will bless our country. Direct our president in the many decisions he has to make in his great responsibility." When Paul ended his prayer, there was a loud AMEN from the president.

The men ate as they were told, respecting the wishes of their country's leader. The meal lasted for about an hour. While they were eating, Paul noticed a number of military men in the next room. They appeared to be waiting for something. He couldn't help but notice the commanding officer who had spoken to them the night before. He had the feeling that all was not well and that they would soon know it.

"My brothers," called the president as he stood to his feet, "as all of you know, we are a country rich in culture. For the past fifty years we have been influenced by foreign political and religious forces. The main religious interference is by the American missionaries." The president stopped a moment as though he wanted to watch the reaction of the men to his last statement. "I will soon order all the American missionaries to leave the country. After they leave, we will need strong national religious leaders to take their place. You men represent that leadership. I am counting on you."

The president then turned and motioned for the commanding officer to come into the room. He walked stiffly up to the chief of state, saluted and turned to face the group of pastors.

"Men, you are our country's spiritual leaders. I regret that you had such ill treatment last night, but we were informed that you were planning an overthrow of the president. Since then we have learned that our source of information was not reliable." The officer gestured now and then toward the president as he spoke. "Our chief of state has honored you men this morning by having breakfast with you. He recognizes your qualities of leadership. All of you have a tremendous influence in your sections of the country, and that is one reason why you are so important to our government. The president needs your help."

The men sat in silence, taking in every word.

"Now, you can continue preaching the Bible, but we want you to do a little more than that. We want you to include with your teachings an emphasis on the importance of obeying the government and its laws. In fact, you are commanded by God to do that." The officer smiled and looked about as though he had scored a victory with this last statement.

"Preach the Bible. Teach your people to obey the laws of the land. In doing so, they will automatically carry out the president's program for cultural revolution. That's all we ask of you men. The president is God's representative among us. We must recognize him in that capacity."

Believing that his speech had convinced the pastors, the officer motioned with his hands for the men to rise to their feet. "All of you who will join with our president to support the cause of the cultural revolution, please stand."

It was strangely silent as everyone in the room rose to his feet—except the thirteen pastors.

II.

Thinking that he had not been understood, the commanding officer repeated his statement. The result was the same. "Do you mean to tell me that you can sit here before our great leader and defy him to his face?"

Turning to Paul, the infuriated officer seemed to spit out the words as he spoke. "Tell your men to get to their feet at once or they will die! Tell them now!"

"Sir," spoke Paul softly but with a steady voice, "we serve Jesus Christ. Our allegiance is to Him and only to Him. We will not compromise the blessed Word of God by mixing with it the teachings of the wicked initiation rites."

"Shoot the fool!" yelled the officer as he raised his fist in Paul's face.

"No," called the president; "let him speak his heart."

"Thank you, Mr. President," said Paul turning to his country's leader. "We love our country and would die for it if necessary. We respect you too, Mr. President, and honor you as our chief of state. The cultural revolution brings back the old ways of living which we left when Christ saved us. The initiation rites, with the blood sacrifices, dances and Satan worship, are sinful. We will not have a part in them. We cannot support your decree of cultural revolution."

"Do all you men feel the same?" questioned the president.

Without exception, every man nodded his agreement with Paul.

47

"Then I must turn you over to my commanding officer. He will punish you for your treason." The president turned and walked from the room.

"Treason!" whispered Paul to himself. "Why, we aren't traitors. We're honest citizens who are standing up for what we believe the Word of God teaches."

Once again the rough treatment began as the soldiers handcuffed the men and herded them into a small courtyard which was surrounded by high walls.

"Line up against that wall over there," commanded the officer in charge. "I want to hear each of you apologize for insulting the president."

Two soldiers appeared, carrying long leather whips which had sharp pieces of steel sticking out of them. "We'll see how much you can take and remain true to your God," sneered the officer. "Don't take off their clothes, men. We'll let the whips do that for us."

Paul cried out as he felt the sting of the leather and steel rip into his back, taking away half his shirt as the whip was pulled back for a second blow. Again and again the cutting blows landed. Blood ran down Paul's naked body. The screams of his fellow pastors seemed muffled by his own intense suffering. Not being able to stand any longer, he slumped to the ground where he was straightened out flat by the steel toe of a military boot.

"Have you had enough, you coward?" Paul looked up with glazed eyes as the commanding officer spit on him. "Take him to the rat cage. That will revive the animal."

The men were dragged to a small concrete building at one end of the court. Inside they were pushed into small individual cells in the concrete floor. Each cell was covered by a steel grate and was constructed in such a way that it was impossible for a prisoner to sit or stand.

"Water them down," commanded the leader.

Immediately a hose was turned on the men, partly filling each cell so that part of their bodies would be submerged.

"Give them the sand treatment," came another order.

From a large barrel, one of the soldiers took tick-infested sand and shoveled it into the faces of the trapped men. Paul wanted to rub the sand from his eyes and face, but he found it impossible to move because of his handcuffs. The soldiers then left the building, leaving the place in total darkness. Paul could hear the groans of the other pastors. The men lost all sense of time in their wretched conditions. They could not tell that two days passed before the soldiers returned.

"Come on, you animals," called the familiar voice. "We're going to take you for a nice long ride."

Their pain was so intense that the dazed men were not conscious of their need for water or food. They were dragged from their cells and stripped of any remaining clothing on their battered bodies. The soldiers then dressed them in the loose fitting robes which were the country's prison garb. Next they were pulled outside and pushed into the back of an army truck. Two days of total darkness caused the light from the rising sun to hurt their eyes. Their bodies were numb from the cold and cramped position into which they had been forced during their time in the floor cells. Fifteen soldiers, armed with automatic rifles, crowded into the truck with the suffering pastors. The soldiers laughed and joked as they sat on top of their prisoners. Now and then a heel or toe of a combat boot would crash into the face of one of the men below.

About an hour from town, the soldiers were surprised to hear singing from the mass of human cargo. One of the pastors sang out as loudly as he could, "Face to face with Christ, my Savior, Face to face, what will it be? When with rapture I behold Him, Jesus Christ who died for me."

"Stop that singing, you fool. Don't you know you are going to be shot?"

"Yes," answered one of the other pastors, "he knows as well as the rest of us. But friend, death doesn't really frighten us. You see, we belong to Christ."

"That's right," added Paul. "Christ means everything to us. He is all we need."

Some of the soldiers seemed disturbed at this show of courage by the bruised and beaten men. The sun was now well above the hills in the east and seemed to add its wrath by focusing its intense heat on the little group of pastors. After more than two hours of traveling, the truck came to a halt. Paul, who knew the country well, recognized the place. It was in an isolated part of the country, thirty miles from the nearest village.

"Pull them out," came the order from the officer in charge.

One by one the men were hauled from the truck and pushed into a clearing. Some found it difficult to stand by themselves. The soldiers lined up in front, holding their weapons ready for their orders.

The leader walked over to Paul, who was trying to help one of the other pastors stand. "All right, Mr. Spokesman, this is it. You have your choice as to life or death."

Silence hung over the two groups of men as the one-sided conversation went on. "I was told to give you one more chance to change your mind. Either you bow down in the name of our president and agree to his cultural revolution, or you will die like animals. Now, my brother, don't be stupid! Accept the president's offer, and we will take you back to your families."

Thirteen lives hung in the balance as Paul prepared to answer. The other pastors seemed perfectly content to have the eighty-year-old spiritual leader represent them. Paul began to speak slowly. "Sir, for many years our people lived in fear, saturated with superstitious beliefs. We worshiped animals, bones, sticks, rivers and many other things. It was only when the missionaries came and told us about Jesus that we heard about the true, living God."

"Go on," spoke the leader. "I want to be able to tell the president that I gave you the chance to say all that you wanted to say." The soldiers stood by quietly, listening to every word. In each of their hearts, they knew that they had to respect such courageous men.

Paul glanced at the officer in charge. "I'm old enough to be the grandfather of your children. I know of what I speak for I was born in this land eighty years ago. I sacrificed chickens and goats to gods that did not see or hear. I taught this same wicked way to many of our people. But then I heard about Jesus, and He changed my life completely. He not only saved me, but also my entire family. He has given us purpose in life. Sir, He means everything to me as well as to my brothers standing here with me."

"I'm not asking you to change your belief," interrupted the officer. "I'm only asking you to honor our national leader by obeying his decree and to show that by bowing down in his name."

"We'll not do that, Sir," answered Paul with a firmness in his voice. "We'll not support his decree of cultural revolution, and we'll not bow down to him. We serve Christ and Christ alone. There is nothing you can do which will make us deny our God." Paul hesitated as he weighed every word he spoke. "We love our precious families, and we realize that we will not see them again until we meet them in Heaven. Our reply to you, Sir, is that we

choose death rather than to deny our God and His holy Word."
As Paul finished speaking, the pastors turned to face the line of
soldiers.

"You fools!" shouted the angry leader. "You deserve to die,
you . . . you animals!" He commanded his men to pick up their
rifles and take aim at their helpless captives. "You've got one
more chance. Will you support the cultural revolution?"

"We will not dishonor God's Word," answered Paul.

"Shoot!" shouted the officer.

The forest echoed with the roar of the rifles, and the terrible
execution was committed. On the ground before the soldiers were
the bleeding bodies of thirteen brave African pastors—men who
chose death rather than to compromise God's Word. A shallow
grave was dug, and the bodies pushed in. In silence the soldiers
took their last look at the spot marked with dried blood where
the spiritual leaders died. Somehow, in their hearts, the soldiers
knew they had committed a horrible crime against the only true
God.

AUTHOR'S NOTE: Shortly after Paul was arrested and probably
already dead, a missionary talked with Elizabeth. Just as her
husband spoke in behalf of his fellow pastors, she spoke in
behalf of the pastors' wives. "Sir," she said with that
ever-pleasant smile on her face, "we realize that we may never
see our husbands again on this side of Heaven. But, Sir, it's really
not a bad thing to die for Jesus Christ." Hearing those words from
Elizabeth, and realizing the grief and heartache of the thirteen
families, the missionary turned his head as tears filled his eyes.
"Truly," he thought to himself, "these people know the real
meaning of dedication and sacrifice."

8

Food for the Crocodiles

"YOU ARE GOING TO DIE because you have taken the side of the missionaries in our struggle to be independent. We have made an oath, sealed by our blood, to cut up your body and feed it to the crocodiles."

Pastor Eli Kepa knew he had enemies because of his uncompromising stand on the Word of God, but he never thought that anyone would threaten to take his life because of it. Eli had just returned to his house from his garden and had found the note fastened to the door of his hut. He knew that the men who wrote the note meant every word they said and that they would carry out their threat as soon as possible.

"Father," he prayed, as he stood looking at the note on the door, "I only want to honor and glorify You. If I am to die for Your name, then help me to die as a brave soldier of the cross."

Reaching up, he took the note, folded it and slipped it into his pocket. "I don't want Marie to know about this."

"Hello, Pastor," called several children walking by. "How are you today?"

Eli looked up from the fire he was building for the evening meal. "I'm fine, thank you," he answered. "Don't forget to come to children's class tomorrow morning. We have something special for you." The pastor was thinking of the overnight trip he and Marie planned to take with their young people.

Within a short time, Eli had a hot fire going. He pulled up a handmade folding chair and sat by the fire, waiting for Marie to return from the garden.

Again the words of the note invaded his thinking. Reaching into his pocket, Eli pulled out the soiled piece of paper and read it over and over again. He was surprised by the sudden appearance of Marie.

"What's wrong, Eli? You look very troubled," asked his faithful companion. Eli and Marie had been married for twenty-five years. Their two daughters, who married brothers, had been gone from their parents' home for six years. Marie, after all these years of marriage, could easily tell when something was on her husband's heart.

Eli knew that he had to share the contents of the note with his wife. "Perhaps it is best that you read it, Marie. I found it fastened to the door when I returned home from the garden this afternoon."

Marie took the note from her husband and began to read the scribbled handwriting. A serious look spread across her face, for she, too, knew that whoever wrote the note meant what he said. Her husband's life was threatened and, humanly speaking, he was doomed to die.

"We serve a great God, Eli," said Marie, handing the note back to her husband. "He can and will protect you. I'm going to ask Him to spare your life so you can give Him more years of service."

As Eli took the note from his wife, he prayed within his heart, "Thank You, Lord, for Marie. Whatever comes out of this, I want Your will to be done."

In spite of the threatening letter he had received that afternoon, Eli and Marie invited the families on each side of them to eat with them that evening. It was a common sight to see several visitors eating with the pastor and his wife in the evening. They loved to have company, and Marie had the reputation of being one of the finest cooks in the area.

After their guests had returned home, Marie and Eli sat by the kerosene lamp in their small house, discussing the message of the note. "I feel sorry for our people," Eli said, looking across the table at Marie. "Why, our missionaries and we pastors have nothing to do with our people obtaining their independence. In fact, if anyone has any independence in this land, it is our Christian population. Every one of our national churches is pastored by a national pastor. Our churches handle their own funds, pay their own pastors, and carry out their own church government. We are independent any way that you look at it."

53

Marie nodded her approval as Eli continued. "Our missionaries have done nothing to us or to our people to merit harm or expulsion from our country. Now, because we pastors defend our missionaries, many of our fellow tribesmen look upon us as traitors."

At last Eli and Marie retired for the night, leaving the matter in God's hands.

Marie opened her eyes and stirred as she heard a nearby rooster crow. Slipping quietly out of bed, she went outside to start the fire and prepare breakfast.

"I have to go to Sarh today," said Eli, as he drank the last drop of coffee from his cup. "The pastors are coming in to talk over this whole situation. It has been brewing for some time now, and we know one man involved in stirring up trouble has spent some time in Russia. I am sure that this so-called nationalistic spirit would not be as explosive if it were not for this outside interference."

Eli was always glad for the opportunity to fellowship with his fellow pastors. He felt the discussions were profitable, and he came away from their meeting determined more than ever before that they needed to take a firm stand on the Word of God and not turn against the missionaries whom God had sent to work among them.

"This road is sure quiet and a lonely place to be this time of the day," thought Eli to himself as he peddled his bicycle toward Balimba. It was only four miles between Balimba and Sarh, but once the sun was down, the road along the river was completely deserted, mainly due to fear and superstitious beliefs by the Sara tribe.

"I'm almost home," whispered Eli as he approached the bridge.

All of a sudden, a man appeared out of the darkness and came toward the pastor. He held a sharp throwing weapon above his head. Eli stopped his bicycle.

"Now I have you," sneered the stranger, waving the weapon in Eli's face. "Did you receive our note? Have you heard of our decision to kill you?" Without giving Eli a chance to answer, he continued, "I'm going to kill you right here and take your head with me to show to my comrades."

The pastor stepped toward the stranger and looked directly into his eyes. "Yes, I received your note. I read how you've threatened to cut up my body and feed it to the crocodiles."

Eli glanced at the nearby river as he spoke. "Here I am. You can take me and kill me. I'll not stop you. Cut me up and feed me to the crocodiles."

The stranger lowered the weapon to his shoulder as Eli continued.

"I belong to the Lord. You can destroy my body, but you can't harm my soul. It is safely secured by my God."

The man stood silently and seemed somewhat bewildered as to what to do. He finally dropped his weapon to his side. "Pastor," he said in a shaky voice, "I was hired to kill you. Never have I seen anyone with such courage. Your God has given you strength to say what you said tonight."

The stranger turned and threw the weapon into the river. "I must go now," he said, "but may I come to your house tomorrow to hear about your God?"

"Of course you can," answered the pastor. "I would like to tell you about Him now."

"No," he answered, looking over his shoulder; "I must go, and you must hurry on home. They may come any minute, and I don't want them to catch us. I will come to your house tomorrow at this same time."

The two men shook hands, and the stranger disappeared into the darkness.

That night as Eli shared with Marie what had happened, a big smile came across her face. "Remember our conversation, Eli?" she asked. "I told you that I was asking God to spare your life for more years of service for Him. Not only has He done this, but you will have the opportunity to witness to the one who was hired to kill you."

In his heart, Eli thanked God for Marie.

9

Beta's Stand

DIANE LOOKED AT MIKE who was sitting across the room at his desk. "Did you say that they would harm you if you returned to their village?" questioned Diane.

Mike stopped typing and turned to his young wife. "That's right, Diane. They told me that we should return to America because they have no use for missionaries or their 'African preacher boys.' "

"What are you going to do, Mike?" asked Diane. "Beta just started the new work there at Jobi."

"That's true," answered Mike, "but his life is in danger. They hate him just like they hate us. I'm afraid if he remains there, someone may try to kill him."

The chills ran up Diane's back. The situation during the past month had become increasingly worse as the communist influence found inroads among the people. Mike Allen knew the cause of all the trouble. The whole thing started when a former military man, called John, arrived in the area. The African grapevine spread the story that John had been to Russia.

"If only that man John would leave, things would return to normal," said Diane.

"You're absolutely correct," agreed Mike. "He's a natural tool for the communists among these people. He belongs to the Sara tribe and is accepted as one of them. There is very little opposition to his spreading poisonous propoganda."

Diane walked to the refrigerator for a drink of water. "Did the people at Jobi mention anything to you about John?"

The hot dry day wore on, and it seemed to Lucy that it would never end. She wondered how much more she could take when a one-year-old baby died in her arms that afternoon. Lucy's body felt drained of all feeling as she walked across the mission compound to her little whitewashed house. She loved her work, but she always appreciated the quietness and relaxing atmosphere of her little dwelling after a hard day's work.

"Miss Lucy! Miss Lucy!" called Rachel, running up to the nurse. "Do you want me to stay with you tonight?"

It was not unusual for the young African girl to stay with Lucy. Many times the two of them would take turns sitting with serious cases during the night.

Lucy smiled at her friend. "Thank you, Rachel, but I don't think we'll have any problems tonight with our patients. I appreciate your thoughtfulness." She watched Rachel until she disappeared over the hill on her way to the village.

As she entered her house, Lucy felt a strange silence. "Where's Antoine?" she asked herself. Antoine had worked for her for ten years as an all-around houseboy. He cleaned the house, chopped wood and even helped with the cooking. She walked into the kitchen and found a note on the table.

"Miss Lucy," she read, "I cannot work for you anymore. It hurts my heart much to write this to you. Our officials say you are a spy. I do not believe this, but I am afraid if I work any longer, they will think I am one heart with you. Please forgive me and please destroy this note. Antoine."

Lucy's heart sank, but she couldn't blame Antoine. "How can they think that about me?" she mumbled to herself. "I love them and have given my life to the Lord to serve them." The hot tears blurred her vision.

Not feeling hungry, Lucy took a quick shower and went to bed. "Rest is more important to me right now than food," she said, as she drifted into a deep sleep.

"Yes, who is it?" called Lucy, more asleep than awake. She opened her eyes as she realized someone was pounding on her front door. She quickly threw on a housecoat and went to the door. Her heart skipped a beat as she opened the door and faced four armed soldiers.

"You're wanted at headquarters immediately," said the leader in a rough-sounding voice.

"All right," answered Lucy. "Please give me time to get dressed."

"Miss Smith, you are a suspect in a spy ring in our country," spoke the officer at the military camp headquarters. "We have questions to ask. Please sit down."

Lucy was glad for the invitation to sit down, as she thought her knees would buckle under her if she remained standing. The questioning continued throughout the night and into the morning. Lucy was tired and hungry. About noon, the officer ordered the men to take her back to the mission station and place her under house arrest.

"You are not to leave your house, and you may not have any visitors. I don't want you to speak to anyone except the guards. Do you understand?" he shouted.

"Yes, Sir," replied Lucy. She couldn't believe this was happening to her.

"Lord, help me to be a testimony to these guards," she prayed that night as she lay in bed. She could hear the guards moving about at the front and back doors.

The days dragged on. She thought of Rachel and the work at the dispensary. Each day the guards would supply her with water, but no mention was made of food. Two weeks passed, and Lucy's food supply was getting low. During the third week her food was gone.

"Dear Father, send me food somehow," she prayed one morning before leaving her bedroom.

One of the guards called her to the back door. Along with the water, he handed her a large gourd of rice and sweet potatoes. "Someone left these on the path near your house," he told her. "I know they're for you."

The hot tears trickled down her face. God had heard and answered her prayer. "Thank You," she said softly.

Each morning without fail she received a gourd full of food. Sometimes there were peanuts, other times beans, and other times a mixture of things. The story of Elijah's being fed by the ravens became a reality to Lucy Smith.

Two months went by. One morning one of the guards told her that they had orders to leave. "You're not a spy," he said, surprising Lucy. "All of us who have been guarding you have learned some wonderful things from you. We have seen your love and patience even though you've been falsely accused. You have shown a concern for our people."

Lucy wondered how they could see this just through guarding her.

"Miss Smith," he continued, "would you please come to our military camp and teach us the Word of God? You could have classes with our wives and our children inside the camp. We'll get you special permission."

Lucy couldn't believe her ears. "Yes," she replied, "I'll be glad to come and hold classes in the camp with your families." Her heart was throbbing with excitement. She gave the men some gospel literature and promised them she would come.

"Thank You, Father," she prayed on her way to the dispensary; "thank You for this open door to teach Your Word in the military camp."

Lucy heard a call and looked up to see Rachel running toward her. Throwing her arms around the missionary, she cried, "Oh, Miss Lucy, I'm so glad to see you. We missed you more than words can tell."

Lucy, too, was glad to be back at her work. The two months had provided a time of rest and had also served as a contact to open the military camp to the gospel. The source of the gourds of food was often in Lucy's thinking. Someday she would mention that miracle to Rachel and Antoine.

11

Kossy's Capture

"DID YOU NOTICE THAT NEW BOY in the youth group today?" called Jerry from the outside storehouse.

Pam looked up from the small flower bed where she was working. "Yes, I talked with him and tried to get some information about him, but he's very shy," replied the young missionary wife. "In fact," she continued, "some of the young people tell me that he just moved here. He's an orphan and lives with Kolo, the witch doctor. They say Kolo is his uncle. Since he is his closest relative, by tribal law he had to live with him."

"What's his name?" asked Jerry.

"He told me his name is Kossy. He has no brothers or sisters," Pam answered.

"Let's call it a day," said Jerry, looking at the setting sun.

"That's fine with me," Pam answered, taking Jerry's hand.

"Mr. Stern, can I see you a minute? I have some good news for you." Jerry turned to see Pastor Mbeti entering the yard.

"Hello, Pastor. What good news do you have for me?"

"Well," answered the pastor, "do you know the new fellow in the next village by the name of Kossy?"

"As a matter of fact, we were just talking about him a few minutes ago. What about him, Mbeti?"

"I just had the joy of leading him to Christ," the pastor said with excitement.

"Praise the Lord!" shouted Jerry. He then turned to the house and called to Pam. "Pam, Pastor Mbeti just told me that he led Kossy to Christ this afternoon."

"Oh, that's wonderful. I've been really praying for him," she said with a big smile.

The pastor told how he had been asked to referee a soccer game that afternoon. Kossy was one of the players and played such an outstanding game that the pastor went to him after the game to comment on his good play. In their conversation, he discovered that Kossy was not a Christian. He witnessed to him, and, as a result, Kossy accepted Christ as his Savior.

"We must pray for Kossy, Mr. Stern," said the pastor. "You see, he lives with Kolo, his uncle, and he doesn't have his tribal scars yet. That is unheard of for a boy his age. I am sure he will be forced to go with the next group of young men in the next Yondo ceremonies."

A thought flashed into Jerry's mind. "Mbeti," he said, "if he would like to have a job here at the mission station, tell him to come and see me." The two men shook hands and parted.

The following morning, Kossy appeared, seeking the job offered to him by Jerry. The job kept him at the mission station during the day and gave him opportunity to attend classes. He matured quickly in the Lord, and everyone had a deep love for him.

One day Kossy approached Jerry. "Mr. Stern," he said in his shy way; "I have a big problem, and I believe the Lord wants me to tell you about it."

"What is it, Kossy?" Jerry looked at the young African and thought how much he had grown in the Lord the past three months.

"Well, Sir, my Uncle Kolo says that I must go to the Yondo initiation rites next week. I really can't go, Sir, because I'm a Christian. I know that he will force me to go if I continue to live with him."

He hesitated a bit and then continued, "Sir, can I come and stay here at the mission station? I'll do anything you ask me to do. You won't even have to pay me. Please, Sir?"

Jerry looked into Kossy's pleading face. "I'll tell you what, Kossy. Mrs. Stern and I will talk it over, and we'll tell you tomorrow. Is that all right?"

Kossy half smiled, "Yes, Sir. That will be fine."

Kossy was overwhelmed the next morning when he was told that he could come and live at the mission station. He hurried home, rolled up his grass bed-mat and tied his clothing in a bundle.

"Where do you think you're going?" growled his uncle as he came into the hut, surprising Kossy.

"I'm going to live at the mission station. Mr. Stern told me I could come and stay with them," stammered Kossy.

His uncle's face showed anger. "You'll do nothing like that, young man," he said, spitting forth the words.

It was hard for Kossy to speak. His mind was confused. He knew that he should obey his uncle, but he also knew that he could not take part in the Yondo rites.

"I am a Christian, Uncle Kolo," he said, "and I can't obey you in this. I must leave. Thank you for all you've done for me. Good-bye, Uncle." Kossy went through the doorway, carrying his bedroll and bundle of clothes.

After Kossy told Jerry what had happened, Jerry warned him never to leave the mission station. He knew that Kossy's uncle would go to any extreme to get him and force him into the Yondo ceremonies. To keep Kossy close at hand, Jerry gave him a job as his yard boy. This kept him away from the outer limits of the mission compound. Each evening Kossy was locked in the outside kitchen. Every precaution was taken to protect him. The Sterns even provided him with much of his food.

Kossy became very close to Jerry and Pam. When they returned to America for furlough, it was difficult for them to leave this "adopted" member of their family. Before he left, Jerry told his replacement about Kossy, and it was decided that the same protection would be given to him.

And then it happened. Kossy was working one day near the edge of the mission compound and was a bit careless as to how close he got to the tall grass. Before he realized it, a man who had been hiding in the grass darted out and quickly took him captive.

The next twelve months were filled with nightmare experiences for Kossy. He was taken to the Yondo camp deep in the jungle. He lived in a small, self-made, grass hut. Rats, leaves, roots, caterpillars, birds and even grass became part of his diet. He was hungry all the time and ate anything he could find. One day he was taken to the Yondo campfire. He was held down while his uncle's helpers carved designs into his forehead, cheeks and back. Writhing in pain, he crawled back to his hut with his wounds filled with ashes and wrapped in leaves. Kossy thought he would die.

When his wounds were sufficiently healed, he was subjected to cruel beatings. The men used bark or grass whips and even wooden clubs. Some of the young people who made it through the tribal designs were either crippled or killed by the terrible beatings. The Lord was very close to Kossy through it all. He was finally released and declared an adult in the tribe.

Meanwhile, Jerry and Pam had had a blessed furlough. The trip back to Africa by freighter had been restful and interesting. They had traveled with their baggage, which included a new pickup truck.

"I can hardly wait to get to the mission station," Pam told Jerry. They were just about a mile away. "We haven't had much communication from anyone."

"Jerry! There's Kossy!" shouted Pam in excitement.

Jerry stuck his head out of the cab window. "Kossy!" called Jerry; "we're back!" The young man didn't respond.

"I'm sure he heard you," said Pam, "and I know it's Kossy."

Jerry called again, "Kossy! We've returned!"

The young man quickly moved away.

"Something is wrong," said Jerry as he pulled the truck beside the fleeing youth. He jumped out and caught him by the arm.

"Hey, Kossy. What's wrong? Remember us? We're your family," Jerry spoke quietly. Kossy still looked the other way.

Jerry took Kossy by the shoulder and turned him around. As he looked at him, he couldn't believe that he was looking at the same young man they had left a year ago. The tribal scars showed clearly.

"Kossy, what happened? You said you didn't want this to happen to you."

Kossy dropped his head and spoke softly, "Mr. Stern, I was too embarrassed to let you see me with these scars." He then told Jerry and Pam what had happened. As he spoke, Pam wiped the tears from her eyes. She realized again how difficult it is for African Christian young people to take a stand for Christ in the face of the popular tribal rites.

"I love the Lord so very much, Mr. Stern, and I believe He wants me to go to Bible school to prepare for His work. I know these scars look terrible, but I'm so thankful that the Lord spared my life to serve Him."

He looked up and smiled, "At least you won't have to feed me and lock me up every night." Then he climbed into the cab to accompany them to the mission station. In his heart he prayed, "Thank You, dear Father, for the safe return of my parents."

Protected by the Lord

"The angel of the LORD encampeth round about them that fear him, and delivereth them" (Ps. 34:7).

12

Invaded by Ants

"MAYBE RAY HAS HAD TROUBLE with his truck," thought Jim as he walked to the front door of the dormitory. He looked down into the valley for any sign of headlights. Jim and Mary, better known as Uncle Jim and Aunt Mary, were beginning their third year as house parents for missionary children at Kaga-Bandoro, a small town in the Central African Empire. Mary watched her husband as he peered off into the darkness, hoping to hear a sound or see some sign of the approaching vehicle which carried its precious load of missionary children.

Early that afternoon, the MK's began arriving. Now all but seven of the forty-six had arrived and were safely under their mosquito nets for the night. Of course, since Ray and Lois had to travel for three days over treacherous roads, almost anything could happen along the way. The diesel generator, which supplied the mission station with lights until 9:30 P.M. each night, had been shut down two hours ago. Mary could see concern written all over Jim's face in the light of the kerosene pressure lamp which they lit after the electricity went off.

As Jim stood and listened, the usual night sounds seemed much louder than normal. Off in the distance, he heard the rapid beats of a village dance drum. Every now and then the sound of the Bible school students singing hymns could be heard. The students liked to get together once a week for a time of fellowship which lasted many times well into the night.

"Jim! Did I hear the sound of a motor?" whispered Mary, who was now standing beside her husband. They both listened, hoping to hear that familiar drone of a motor off in the distance. "Yes, I do hear a motor," said Jim, "and it is coming from the south too."

Within minutes the headlights could be seen as the truck approached the Baptist Mid-Missions' station where the school for MK's was located. Kaga-Bandoro was a typical Central African town, consisting of a few small stores, a post office and a government post.

Ray pulled up in front of the dorm. "Hi, Ray!" called Jim. "Did you have trouble?"

"I sure did," answered Ray, stepping from the cab. "I blew three tires over the last hundred miles. Some of those rocks are as sharp as knives."

Flashlights seemed to appear out of nowhere as the MK's began unloading their baggage from the back of the truck. Everyone was tired from the long trip, and it was a welcome sound when Aunt Mary called, "Food's ready. Come and get it." She knew there would be a truckload of hungry people, and she had the food ready and waiting for them.

"Boy, that was good, Aunt Mary," said Paul, who was in his last year of school. "I sure love your banana cream pie."

"So do I," said Ray, winking at Lois as he finished his second piece.

Because of the lateness of the hour, everyone pitched in to help Aunt Mary clear the table and do the dishes. Showers were taken in record time, and soon all were in their beds awaiting the first day of school.

Jim was just drifting off to sleep when he heard the voice of his daughter Sue. "Dad, are you awake?" she called softly.

"Yes, Sue, I'm awake. What do you want?"

Sue, not wanting to make too much noise, opened the bedroom door a crack. "Dad, please come. There are ants all over our bedroom."

Mary, who was wide awake by this time, pulled her flashlight from under her pillow. Handing it to Jim, she said, "You had better go, Dear, and see what the problem is."

Lifting the mosquito net, Jim slipped out of bed. He carefully emptied his shoes before putting them on. He quickly made his way through the dining room and down the hallway of the girls' end of the dormitory. Reaching the room where Sue and Barb slept, he flashed his light inside. He could hardly believe what met his eyes. The walls, ceilings and most of the floor were covered with thousands of flesh-eating red driver ants.

"Barb, are you all right?" asked Jim, looking over at Barb, sitting up in bed.

"Yes, Uncle Jim," answered Barb. "I'm all right, but I am a bit scared."

"There is nothing to be afraid of, Barb," Jim continued, "as long as you stay inside your net."

"Don't worry," grinned Barb. "I don't plan on going anywhere tonight." The other girls were awake by this time and laughed at Barb's remark.

"Uncle Jim, the ants are in our room too," called Karen from across the hall.

A few steps away, Jim saw the same unbelievable sight. Ants were everywhere. A quick glance into the third and last room revealed the same picture.

"They are taking over the hall, Dad!" cried out Sue, who was already retreating to the safety of the dining room.

Jim's heart skipped a beat as he saw a large scorpion fall from the ceiling, just missing Sue's shoulder. The ants were already at work as Jim heard the lizards scurrying on the ceiling, fleeing from the ants.

Jim and Mary had read of ant invasions where whole villages had to be vacated for a short time, but they never dreamed that such would be their experience. "Actually," thought Jim to himself, "our girls, for the time being, are trapped by the ants and must stay in their beds." Jim quickly made his way to the dining room, calling to the girls to stay under their nets. If they needed him for some reason, they were to call him.

Jim and Mary both realized that their family of MK's was a unique family. Most of the young people spent most of their lives in Africa and were not easily frightened with such experiences.

"Lord, take care of our family," prayed Jim as he lay quietly in bed, listening for a call from one of the young people. Sleep finally overcame him. The next thing he knew he was looking at his watch which read five o'clock. "The kids!" thought Jim as he lifted the net and looked at the floor for ants. The flashlight showed none, and Jim quickly dressed, once again emptying his shoes before putting them on. Being careful with every step, he walked into the dining room and started down the hall. The quietness led Jim to believe that the MK family was sound asleep. A quick look around the dorm told Jim that the worst of the invasion was over. In fact, even though there were thousands of ants still present, one could see that they were only cleaning up the remains of their hunt. They all seemed to be carrying off pieces of scorpions, centipedes and cockroaches.

Just then Jim froze in his tracks as he heard Mary cry out. He turned and raced down the hall, through the dining room and into their bedroom. "What's wrong, Mary? Where are you?" called Jim excitedly.

"I'm here, Jim," answered Mary quietly but with a nervous voice. "Jim, look down by my feet," said Mary standing still.

He took one look and gasped. There stretched out on the bathroom floor for about six feet was a black spitting cobra snake, a snake which not only bites but also spits its venom. "Don't move," said Jim, approaching quietly. Taking a good look at the snake, he saw that it was the victim of the driver ants. They had already destroyed its eyes, thus blinding it. "Step back very easy, Mary," Jim directed her. "The snake is blind and can't see you."

Mary backed away as instructed by her husband. Jim found a long pole; then, standing at a safe distance, he nudged the snake. Like a flash of lightning, the cobra swung its head high and opened its mouth to strike. The pole came down upon its head time and time again until the snake lay harmless on the floor.

"Boy, that was a close one!" said Mary. "I'm sorry I yelled like I did, but it really scared me when I looked down to see it only about ten inches from my feet."

"Well, praise the Lord for the ant invasion!" said Jim with a big thankful smile.

"Praise the Lord for the ant invasion?" questioned Mary. "What do you mean?" A puzzled look spread across her face.

"Well you see," replied Jim, "that snake was living somewhere in the girls' end of the dormitory, and the ants found it. They chased it and finally cornered it here in our bathroom where they finally got the best of it."

"I see," said Mary. "That snake could have bitten one of the girls if it had not been found. Isn't it wonderful how the Lord looks after us?"

That day at school the classrooms buzzed with excitement as each student told his or her version of the night before. That evening during devotions, one of the fellows prayed, "Lord, if there is a snake in our end of the dormitory, please send us an ant invasion."

Listening to this sincere prayer by one of their MK's, Mary could not help but smile.

13

The Hunt

"THERE IS ONE VILLAGE I wish we could reach with the gospel," mused Darrell as he turned his head to look out the pickup truck window. "And to think that it's the closest village to our mission station on this road."

Peggy Rice knew what her husband was thinking, for they had prayed together many times for the village of Kouma. "We'll just keep praying, Honey. One of these days the Lord will use something to open Kouma for the gospel."

The small, bush mission station of Kyabe, in the Republic of Chad, had been opened only ten years before as an outreach to the primitive Sara Kaba tribe, famous for its disc-lipped women. Darrell and Peggy Rice were in the final year of their first term.

Darrell drove in silence, thinking about the nearby village. He turned to Peggy, "Let's pray for Kouma right now."

"Dear Father," Peggy prayed as they rode along, "help us to reach the people of Kouma with Your Word. They seem to be so indifferent and even refuse to gather for us when we go there." Peggy's voice then broke with a sob. "Lord, we don't know of one Christian in the entire village. Please use us to break down that wall of opposition before we leave for our furlough next June."

That night after the evening meal, Darrell read the Bible and prayed with Peggy and the children. Five-year-old Tammie sat beside her daddy while Peggy held one-year-old Mark. Again the young couple prayed specifically for the village of Kouma where there seemed to be a stiff resistance to the gospel.

It was a week later, during the midday two-hour break

period for the workmen, that a group of six men walked onto the mission station. They were armed with spears, knives and machetes and were dressed only in loincloths. The scars on their faces and chests showed that they belonged to the Sara Kaba tribe. The six tall men made their way to the Rice home.

Darrell had just stretched out on his bed for a fifteen-minute rest before going out to the garage to work on his truck. The silence was broken by hand clapping. This was the African way of calling the occupants of a house to the door.

Peggy, who had just entered the bedroom, heard the clapping and looked out through the screened window. She hurried to Darrell's side. "Darrell, there are six men in the backyard armed with spears and knives. They may be friendly, but they sure don't look like it."

Darrell hurried to the window to look at the men. He recognized two of them as men he had seen at Kouma. "Hello there," Darrell called. "Welcome to the mission station. I'll be right out." He made his way quickly to the backyard. "Father," he prayed as he went, "use this contact to open Kouma to the gospel."

Stepping off the back porch with a big smile, he began shaking their hands, which was always a sign of friendship. The men responded with handshakes and smiles, showing their filed, pointed teeth.

"What can I do for you?" Darrell asked the man who was standing in front of the group and acting as their leader. The tall, scarred-faced African looked at Darrell with his bloodshot eyes and began to speak. Immediately Darrell recognized that the leader, and no doubt the other five, had been drinking "native beer."

"Well, it's like this," said the leader; "we're hungry. Our people are hungry. And we'd like you to go hunting with us today. The reason we came now is that we spotted fresh warthog tracks in the cotton gardens alongside the mission station. We're asking you to take your gun and go with us."

Instead of answering their question immediately, Darrell looked at the leader. "Aren't you Saley?" Darrell remembered that Pastor Luke, the station pastor, had mentioned the name of Saley to him one time as the leader at Kouma.

Saley smiled widely, showing his rotting, pointed teeth. "Yes, I'm Saley. How do you know me?" He turned to his companions, "Look, the white man knows us already." And with this they all nodded approvingly.

Darrell continued, "Well, I heard of you, Saley, and I'll be glad to go hunting with you."

As Darrell shared the good news with Peggy, he was so excited he had difficulty fastening his cartridge belt around his waist. "Rifle, shells, knife, water, sun helmet," Darrell made a mental check as they headed off into the cotton gardens.

The expert hunters soon picked up the trail of the warthog. It was the rainy season, and some of the elephant grass already reached a height of ten to fifteen feet. Darrell had always told Peggy he wouldn't hunt in the high grass during the rainy season. In twenty minutes' time the tracks led out of the garden into the forest. The men stopped. Darrell looked at the uninviting, thick, high grass ahead of him.

"Well, men," he said to the disappointed hunters, "let's plan on hunting another time."

Saley spoke up, "Sir, there are six of us. Trust us, and we'll protect you. Now, will you go with us after the warthog?"

"Father," Darrell prayed silently in his heart, "help me to make the right decision."

"Sir," continued Saley, "we'll put three men in front of you and three men behind you."

Darrell couldn't refuse. He didn't want to miss this opportunity to gain the confidence of these men. "OK, let's go," he said, as the men smiled at each other. Never had he seen grass so high and thick. It was impossible to see more than ten feet on either side.

After about twenty minutes into the grass, Saley stopped. There in front of them was a huge anthill about fifteen feet high and thirty-five feet across. "Sir," Saley said, "that's where the pig lives. Do you see that big tree growing out of the top of the anthill?" Darrell looked and nodded. "Well, beneath that tree," continued Saley, "there's a hole, and I'm sure we'll find the pig there."

The anthill was steep to climb, but Darrell made it without too much trouble. Saley led the way as the two men carefully made their way to the big tree. The other five men remained below in the grass. Saley leaned his spear against the tree and told Darrell that he would see if the pig was in the hole. He got down on his stomach and began to crawl around the base of the tree.

Darrell didn't want to miss anything; so he moved quietly

behind Saley, looking over his shoulder. From up above he could see more than Saley could from his low position. The African moved ahead with caution, inch by inch. Darrell's heart leaped as he began to see a set of sharp tusks move slowly out of the opening of the hole. It was too late to warn Saley. In a few seconds the warthog's nose and Saley's face almost touched. They were only six inches apart. When the hog saw the African, he slipped back into the hole. Saley looked up wide-eyed and whispered, "He's home!"

Saley then stood behind the tree to give Darrell his instructions. "Move in front of the hole. Put the end of the gun in the pig's face and shoot."

Darrell could hardly believe what he was hearing, but he didn't want to back out. Slowly he put the end of the barrel where he had last seen the pig's head. He began to move inch by inch around the tree to the front. The pig's face came into view. Darrell glanced quickly at Saley and saw that Saley was not completely satisfied with his position. He motioned for Darrell to move farther in front of the tree. Darrell soon found himself standing in front of the wild warthog, with the barrel of his gun just two feet away from its head.

"What's going to happen when I pull this trigger?" wondered Darrell. But before he could shoot, the hog grunted loudly and charged.

In self-defense Darrell fired the gun, hitting the base of the tree. He threw his right leg as high as he could as the pig ran under it. In doing so, he fell to the ground on his back. An instant later Saley was bending over him, asking if he was hurt.

"No, he never touched me. I'm all right. But what do we do now?"

"Sir," said Saley, with a serious look on his face, "you've proven that you do care for us. We're your friends. We've had enough for one day. Let's go home. There are many more days in the future for us to get together."

"Thank You, dear Father," Darrell prayed as he lay on the ground. "Thank You for this contact with these people."

A week later, Darrell and Peggy Rice were excited as they paid their third visit to Kouma. Saley, Nabia and Ndjokai, three of the six hunters, had already received Christ as their Savior. The missionaries planned to begin a children's class soon. God had answered their prayers. Kouma was now open to the gospel.

14

Kembe Fights for His Life

"I'M TELLING YOU to stay away from him," said Kim's father as his heart swelled with anger. "Don't you ever go near that fanatic."

"But Father, I . . ." answered the teenage boy.

"Don't give me any of your mouth, Kim," interrupted his father, who seemed to spit out the words. "That pastor's garbage won't get you anything in life. Just stay away from him and don't talk about that stuff to me."

Kim Togo was big for fifteen. Because he was the oldest and biggest of the three Togo sons, he had the responsibility of hunting with his father. Some buffalo had been near the gardens lately, and Kim's father, Kembe, hoped they would be able to kill such a prize. Kim walked silently behind his father, thinking of his burning words.

"Pay attention where you step," warned Kembe. "Any noise now could cost us an animal."

Kim knew what his father meant. The snap of a stick could easily give them away. "I'll be careful, Father," answered Kim.

It was difficult for the boy to keep his mind on hunting after hearing such an outburst from his father. "Why," he thought to himself, "Pastor Mark is such a friendly man, and he does show a lot of love for all of us."

Kim thought of the day he stayed after class to talk with Mrs. Mark about Jesus. He recalled how she prayed with him when he asked Jesus to be his Savior. "And that's where it all started," Kim said under his breath. He remembered how he hurried home to tell his mother and father that he had accepted Jesus. He could almost hear his father's words: "Don't you ever mention that Name in this house again. We have our own gods, and we will worship them."

Kembe stopped abruptly and knelt down to examine some tracks. "It's a pig and a big one at that," he whispered more to himself than to Kim. Carefully he picked the leaves off the tracks. Kim knelt beside his father for a better look.

"It just passed through here, Kim," said his father. "We'll follow the beast."

The two walked slowly through the dried leaves, which seemed to announce their coming. It was impossible not to make noise. Kembe stepped over what he thought was a fallen log covered with leaves. In a flash the "log" came alive. Before the African could defend himself, a large, brown, shiny head leaped out of the leaves. With its mouth wide open, the giant python sent its many needlelike teeth into the calf of the hunter's leg.

"Watch out, Father!" shouted Kim.

Within seconds the huge snake threw two coils around Kembe's body while holding fast with a tight grip on his leg. The two began a battle for life as the leaves flew in all directions. "Go get help! Go get help!" called Kembe to his son.

Kim turned and ran at top speed in the direction of the village.

The twenty-five-foot constrictor put a third coil around Kembe, but not before the husky hunter was able to tear the snake's head from his leg, leaving two deep gashes oozing with blood. Knowing that his life was at stake, Kembe held the python's neck, squeezing as hard as he possibly could and bending it back and forth, trying to break its back.

Kim ran like he had never run before. He knew the jungle well and was able to head straight for the village. "Dear God," he prayed, "save my father's life. Please get help for him." The tears began to blur Kim's vision.

"Kim! Kim!" came a call from among the trees. Kim turned to see Pastor Mark with a large bundle of bark on his head. He was putting a new grass roof on his house and was out gathering bark which he used for tying the grass to the roof poles.

"Oh, Pastor," cried Kim, "come with me. My father has been caught by a python. He might already be dead."

The pastor threw the bark on the ground and raced after Kim through the underbrush. Because of their haste, the branches tore their clothing and scratched their bodies, but there was no time to lose. The two men ran without speaking until they were nearly there; then Kim broke the silence. "He's just on the other side of that high grass," gasped Kim, out of breath.

Pastor Mark took his knife from its sheath, knowing what he had to do. As he came around the edge of the tall elephant grass, he spotted Kembe on the ground with the python tightening its coils around his body.

Kembe tried to speak, but no voice was heard. The snake had gained the upper hand in the battle, and it was just a matter of time as to the outcome.

"Hold on, Kembe," shouted Pastor Mark as he jumped into action. Dodging the python's head which was now free and trying to bite him, the pastor lunged forward, thrusting his knife into the snake's neck. Again and again he stabbed the knife into the twisting, turning serpent. The snake struck at the African pastor, but he was too quick for the wounded python. His sharp knife caught it alongside the head, opening a wide cut.

Kim was afraid to use his knife for fear he might cut his father or the pastor. He finally did find an opportunity and picked up his father's spear. With all his strength, he sent it hurling into the snake, pinning the eight-inch-thick body to the ground.

The battle was over. The snake loosened its coils on Kembe, who was covered with the snake's blood. To make sure that the dying creature couldn't do any more harm to them, Pastor Mark cut a piece of vine and looped it around the snake's head. He then fastened the head securely to a nearby tree.

"Are you all right, my friend?" asked the pastor, kneeling beside Kembe.

"I'll be all right in a few minutes. You came just in time. I thought I was going to die."

Kim uncoiled the snake's body from around his father. "Pastor Mark was out in the jungle when I found him, Father. I prayed that God would. . . ." He stopped, remembering that his father had warned him to not say anything more about God.

"What were you going to say, Kim?" questioned the pastor as he cared for Kembe's leg wound.

"Oh, nothing important," answered Kim. He then handed his undershirt to Pastor Mark to wrap around his father's leg.

"Yes, it is important, Kim," spoke his father, who was rapidly recovering from his battle with the python. "You were going to say that you prayed that your God would send help. Am I correct, Kim?" asked Kembe, looking up at his son.

"Yes, Father, you are correct," responded Kim. "I was afraid that if I had to go all the way to the village for help, I wouldn't have arrived back in time. I asked God to get us help right away, and He did just that Father. He made Pastor Mark come into the jungle this morning to gather bark. Don't you see, Father, that the God I love and serve hears me when I talk to Him, and He answers my prayers?"

"Your son's right, Kembe," said the pastor. "God did this for you. He spared your life. Your gods couldn't do one thing to help you, but my God sent me into the jungle so that I would be here to help you. You see," the pastor continued, "God's answer was on the way even before you got caught by the python."

Kembe looked into Pastor Mark's face. "You are right, Pastor. God did spare my life." He then lifted himself into a sitting position. "Will you help me thank God for doing this for me?" he asked. "Would you show me how Jesus can become my Savior too?"

Kim's heart leaped within him as he listened to his father's words.

The three Africans bowed their heads as Kembe asked God to forgive him of his sins and to save him.

As he was helped to his feet, Kembe looked at the dead snake. "I once heard Kim telling his two brothers about a big fish that God used to give one of His workers directions." A smile spread across his face. "Wait till they hear that God used a big snake to cause their father to accept Jesus."

Kim knew that things were going to be different from now on in the Togo family.

15

Safe at Last

THE HUGE COLUMNS OF BLACK SMOKE reached like fingers into the bright blue sky. Dan could see in the distance the hawks flying low over the burning brush. Now and then one would swoop down to the ground to snatch a fleeing rat or perhaps a dazed lizard. He could see the flames leaping high above the trees. Never was he so scared in all his life. He turned to his African companion, who stood studying the pattern of the fire's approach. "What shall we do now, Bissi? It looks like we are trapped between the fire and the river."

Dan recalled how, that morning at breakfast, his father told him to be extra careful if he planned to go anywhere in the forest. "This is the week for the annual fire hunt, and the workmen tell me that it possibly could be today."

Young Dan knew all about the annual fire. He had often gone with his father to some safe spot to observe the advancing red army as it left its destruction behind it. "I'll be careful, Dad," said Dan. "Bissi wants me to check his traps with him, but he told me that we'll go right after breakfast and check only the three nearest ones."

"We'll just go to the first three traps like I told you yesterday, Dan," said Bissi. "The other four are too far out in the forest. I suppose we could make those, too, if we hurried, but I remember too well what happened last year." Bissi was referring to two nearby villagers who died as they tried to get some honey before the fire reached it.

The boys made good time as they walked to the traps. Bissi

was disappointed that they contained no game. "Let's go see the fourth trap, Dan," the young African had said. "I don't see any smoke in the sky yet, which means that they haven't started the fire."

They were about halfway to the trap when they had noticed the smoke. Someone had set fire to the grass at the mission compound, probably to make a firebreak around the mission property. The red and orange monster spread rapidly, blocking all ways of escape for Dan and Bissi. The boys had retreated farther and farther into the forest until they found themselves approaching the river.

Bissi looked at his American friend. "We are going to have to get into the river, Dan. I know it's filled with crocodiles, but we don't have a choice." Dan shivered at the thought. Bissi knew his friend was afraid. "Come on, Dan. I have an idea. Help build a cage for us."

"A cage! Bissi, do you know what you're saying?"

With Dan close behind, Bissi ran the remaining hundred yards to the riverbank. Dan took a look at the vast body of water and froze in his tracks. As far as he could see up and down the river, crocodiles were lazily floating on top of the water. The fire was driving all kinds of animals into the river for protection. Instead of finding a haven, the plunge turned out to be death in the powerful jaws of the crocodiles.

"Hurry, Dan, we haven't much time," said the young African as he began to cut some bamboo into ten-foot lengths.

Dan followed suit and started chopping as fast as he could swing his machete. The pile of poles quickly grew as the boys feverishly worked.

"While you finish cutting the poles, I'll get some bark to use as rope," said Bissi, running into a nearby thicket.

Within a short time, the boys built a four-sided bamboo cage about ten feet high. Following Bissi's instruction, they slipped it over the bank and into the water.

"You have to get in, Dan, and you must do it now." Bissi managed a smile to try to encourage his American friend. "Let's go, Dan," called Bissi as he leaped into the top of the cage. The slender African sunk to the bottom and then bobbed to the top like a cork.

Dan saw a large crocodile push its nose up against the bamboo poles not more than two feet from Bissi. The fire had reached the riverbank in several places and was quickly approaching the spot where Dan stood. "Lord," he prayed, "save us from the fire and the crocodiles." Without hesitating any longer, he jumped into the cage.

"Hang on to the back wall of the cage, Dan," yelled Bissi. "Don't get near the other three sides."

As Bissi gave instructions to Dan, he worked at tying the crude bamboo cage with bark rope to the roots which stuck out of the water. This made the cage more stable and secure. Within minutes the fire was upon them. All kinds of small animals were jumping off the bank like little divers. Now and then a large splash would tell the boys that a larger animal had just jumped to its death among the waiting crocodiles. The large angry flames leaped out over the heads of the two boys as they clung to the cage.

"Get low in the water," called Bissi. "Stay under as long as you can."

Each time Dan came up for air, he thought the fire was bigger and hotter. One thing which made him feel a bit better was that the fire drove the crocodiles away from the cage and toward the center of the river to wait for their prey.

Finally Bissi looked at Dan and smiled. "We can get out, Dan. There's no danger now from the fire."

Dan quickly climbed over the top of the cage onto the riverbank. He turned to look at the bamboo shelter that had saved their lives. Not more than six feet from the structure three huge crocodiles were moving in fast. How thankful he was that they were now on the bank and that their lives had been spared.

"Dan, I must tell you something," said Bissi, somewhat surprising Dan with the seriousness in his voice.

The American looked at his friend, whom he had known for about two years. "What is it, Bissi?"

"Well, I don't know how to begin," said Bissi as he hesitated. "You see, I've known about Jesus and what He did for me ever since my parents moved to the village next to the mission compound. Because we lived so close, I began to attend teen classes. You remember, Dan? That's where we first met."

"I remember, Bissi," said Dan, listening closely to what his friend had to say.

"Well, what I'm trying to say is that I've never really accepted Jesus. The fire, as well as the crocodiles, could have taken both our lives, but the cage saved us."

Dan hardly knew what to say to his friend. "You're right.

The cage was like Jesus, only He saves us for eternity." The tears trickled out of Dan's eyes and ran down his face.

"Dan," said Bissi, "would you pray with me? Would you help me say the right words to ask Jesus to come into my heart?"

"I'll be glad to pray with you, Bissi," responded Dan with emotion in his voice.

The two boys bowed their heads and prayed as Bissi asked Christ to forgive him of his sins and save him. It was a happy but concerned pair of teenage boys who made their way toward home. Walking was much easier, and they made good time. Before long, they heard someone calling their names.

"They're calling from that direction," said Dan with excitement. Soon they were joined by Pastor Daniel and one of the church deacons.

"Your father is right behind us, Dan," said the happy pastor. "He'll be glad to see you."

Dan could see the distraught look on his father's face disappear as he ran to him. "Dad, I'm sorry I've caused you and Mom to worry. We really didn't mean to go that far. We would have made it back, but the fire started behind us and made it impossible for us to return."

Tom Kemp put his arms around Dan. "Thank the Lord that you boys are safe. We thought you were trapped in the fire. One of the workmen started the back fire by mistake. He didn't know you boys were in the forest."

"Well, Mr. Kemp," spoke up Bissi, "if it hadn't been for that fire, I wouldn't know Jesus as my Savior right now."

The boys explained what had happened to them and the decision that Bissi made after they came out of the river. The veteran missionary reached out and hugged the two boys. "Let's hurry on home, boys." He looked at Dan. "Your mother is waiting to hear that you both are safe." He turned to Bissi and smiled. "I mean *really* safe."

16

Blinded!

LYNN THOUGHT SHE WAS DREAMING. She turned over
to go back to sleep when once again the voice called out in the
still night: "Fire! Fire! The dispensary's on fire!"

There was no mistake about it. Someone was calling to
awaken the villagers. She grabbed her flashlight from under her
pillow and bounded out from under the mosquito net. Running
to the window, she saw the long, flaming tongues of fire leaping
high into the night sky. Throwing a robe around her, she dashed
out the door and ran toward her dispensary. She realized as she
got closer that it was not the dispensary building, but rather one
of the patient's huts directly behind it.

"It's Sesse! It's the blind man!" someone yelled in the crowd
that had gathered. Fear struck her heart as she thought of Sesse
and Bira trapped in that raging furnace.

"Lord," she prayed on the run, "protect those two Arab
boys."

Rounding the corner of the dispensary, she saw the remains
of the little grass hut—a pile of red embers. As she approached
the burning remains, the red glow cast an eerie shadow upon the
strangely silent crowd. Her eyes searched for Sesse and Bira in
the semidarkness.

"Here they are, Miss Ryan," called someone from a group
standing nearby. "They're sitting over here."

"Sesse! Bira! Are you all right?" asked Lynn softly.

"We're all right, Miss Ryan. Our kerosene lantern tipped
over and caught the grass on fire," said Bira.

Seeing the frightened look on the boys' faces reminded Lynn of the day she first met Sesse and Bira. They had come seeking medical help from Lynn Ryan, a missionary nurse in the Central African Empire. How ugly were Sesse's wounds! The sight had almost caused Lynn to be sick. A leopard had attacked Sesse while he was hunting, clawing out both eyes as well as leaving several deep gashes in his scalp. To worsen matters, it had taken two days for Bira to lead his young friend through the forest to the mission station.

Lynn had quickly called Earl Monroe, the station supervisor, and Sesse was rushed to the nearby government hospital. For several days Sesse's life had been of great concern to the French doctor and the missionaries. At last his condition had improved, enabling him to return to the mission station for further recuperation.

"The fire's out now, Miss Ryan. It won't do any more harm," spoke Moses, one of the believers.

Lynn stirred from her thoughts and called to the boys. "Come with me. I'll put up two cots in my workroom. You can stay the rest of the night."

Earl arrived as Lynn and the two boys reached the dispensary veranda. "I'm going to put them up here in the dispensary, Earl. Tomorrow I can find other arrangements for them."

"Let me help you," answered Earl. "I'm sure sorry to see you lose one of those huts."

"That was a close call for you tonight, Bira," said Lynn as she pushed some small boxes aside to make room for the cots.

"I don't even like to think of it, Miss Ryan. I've never been so close to death." Fear seemed to leap out of Bira's eyes as he spoke.

"Me too," chimed in Sesse, who sat quietly on a box, listening to what was being said. "I felt that terrible heat, and I thought it was the end for me."

"Can you imagine what Hell must be like, Sesse?" asked Earl. "The Bible says, 'For the wages of sin is death.' " The room grew silent as the two young men listened. Earl continued, " 'But the gift of God is eternal life through Jesus Christ.' He's the only way to Heaven, fellows. Christ died to save you from paying the penalty for your sins."

"I'm sorry, Mr. Monroe, but I can't believe what you're saying." Sesse reached to his elbow and took hold of the small leather pouch that was fastened there. "You see," he continued, "this is my god. It was this that kept the leopard from killing me. And now, tonight, it was this that spared my life in the fire."

"That's right," added Bira. "We like your medicine and good care, but we can't accept your God."

Earl and Lynn gazed at each other in amazement. Never before had they heard such defiant words—and especially from anyone who had gone through as much as these two young men.

The next two weeks seemed to pass rapidly. As Sesse's physical problem subsided, the more his heart became hardened to the gospel. The day before he and Bira were to leave, Lynn sat down to talk to them.

"Please, Miss Ryan," said Sesse politely, but firmly, "I don't want to hear anymore about your Jesus. I know He means everything to you, but He means nothing to me."

"The same goes for me," added Bira, who sat twisting a piece of grass between his fingers. "He is your God, not ours. We have our own god to worship."

Lynn was stunned at the open rebellion of the two young men. "Surely," she thought to herself, "they can see Christ in us missionaries. I'm sure they see a difference between the believers and the unbelievers." Bidding the men good night, she headed back to her little cottage.

That night in the missionaries' prayer meeting, much time was spent in prayer for Sesse and Bira. There was not a dry eye as the missionaries unburdened their hearts for the Arab men. "They'll be leaving us tomorrow, Lord," prayed Earl. "May they come to You before they return to their village."

The morning sun shone brightly on the small group of people gathered at the mission dispensary. Bira and Sesse did not realize they had made so many friends among the believers. Some of the people even gave part of their food supply to their two friends so they would have something to eat on their way back home. Earl and Lynn stood listening to the chatter.

"Dear friends," called Earl, "let's bow our heads and pray for Bira and Sesse as they leave us."

Lynn watched as Bira and sightless Sesse bowed their heads.

"And dear Lord," prayed the missionary, "we ask You to work in the hearts of Bira and Sesse that they, too, may come to know You as their Savior. They know we love them, Father, but we all want them to recognize Your love for them through Your Son, Jesus."

The Christians stood in line to shake hands with their Arab friends. Lynn and Earl took their places at the end of the line. It was touching to hear the believers assure Bira and Sesse of their continued prayers for them.

Lynn turned to Earl. "These believers have never taken to anyone like they have these two Arabs. It's hard to believe that they are not yet saved."

"I know," responded Earl. "Maybe this close friendship will be used of the Lord to open the door for the gospel in their village."

The two missionaries finally reached their two parting friends. As they shook hands, Bira smiled and spoke. "Please don't think that we are not thankful for your kindness to us." He stopped a moment as though he had to think what he wanted to say next. "It is just that we don't want or need your Jesus. We can't believe that He is God's Son."

Bira's words cut like knives into the hearts of the Christians. Bira's and Sesse's opposition to the gospel only challenged their friends to pray even more for them.

"Mr. Monroe," said Sesse, "my father is the chief of our village, and I know that he would want you to come to see him. In fact, you can even preach about your Jesus if you want to; but I warn you, it won't do any good. Because of what your missionaries did for me, you are welcome to come among my people any time. I can promise you a welcome through my father's authority."

The two men made their way to the main road and started the long trek to their village. "Good-bye," called Bira, waving his hand. "Good-bye, everyone," echoed Sesse.

"Sesse will only suffer in this world for his physical blindness, but think of the torment he will endure for his spiritual blidness," mused Lynn as she watched them go down the road.

"We gave them the Light, Lynn, but they went away in darkness," spoke Earl as he turned to go back to the house. Already he was looking forward to the dry season and his first trip to the Arab village.

17

Ordered by the Lord

TOM DESPERATELY GRABBED for the overturned dugout canoe. The feel of solid wood in his hand felt good. "Thank You, Lord," he gasped as he took hold with his other hand. The swiftly moving water carried him rapidly downstream. "I wonder where Pierre is," he frantically said to himself. His eyes made a quick sweep of the foaming death trap. "Father," he prayed out loud, "save Pierre. Please save him."

That morning when Tom and Pierre left the mission station for their two-day trip to the mission station at Mara, little did they realize the disaster that was ahead of them before the day would end. Tom Bentley was just like any other MK (missionary kid) who lived in the heart of Africa. The land, its people, their language and culture represented a great challenge to him. His eighteen years of living close to the nationals taught him many valuable lessons which one could not learn in a classroom. He loved the outdoors and enjoyed going places and doing things with his Christian African friends. One of his closest friends was Pierre Koli. He practically grew up with Tom. As children, the two had spent hours each day playing together. Tom still had the first truck which Pierre taught him how to make from the heavy, thick elephant grass.

As they became older, they often ventured into the nearby forests, looking for small game with Tom's rifle. He and Pierre wanted to make the two-day trip to Mara by dugout canoe since Tom would soon be leaving for the States.

Over the years, Bud and Mary Bentley had hoped their only

child would go to Bible college and prepare for the Lord's work. Whenever the subject would come up, Tom was quick to tell them that he was interested only in television and wanted to train for commercial TV. At times, he would even become angry with them if they mentioned Bible school.

"Pierre!" shouted Tom as he clung tightly to the canoe. "Pierre! Can you hear me?" Only the roar of the water seemed to answer Tom's call.

Unknown to Tom, Pierre had been thrown out of the canoe and had struck his head on a jagged rock. It was only a miracle that kept him from losing consciousness and slipping under the water. The blow stunned him momentarily, but when he regained his thinking, he found himself clinging to a large log which seemed to appear from nowhere.

"Pierre!" Tom called again. "Can you hear me?" Are you all right?" Tom could hear his echo rebound from the deep forest.

A sudden jerk of the dugout canoe told Tom that he was not moving. The canoe rammed into a thicket of overhanging bushes. He was surprised to find that his feet could touch bottom. Still holding to the canoe, Tom slowly made his way to the stream's bank and pulled himself up by the vines growing along the water's edge. Safely on the bank, Tom scanned the stream in both directions for his faithful companion.

Tom's heart leaped within him as he spotted something downstream below the rapids. He wasn't sure if he saw an arm around a floating log or if his eyes were playing tricks on him. The young American ran along the bank trying to get a better view between the trees and grass which grew alongside the stream.

"Pierre! Is that you?" Tom shouted, cupping his hands over his mouth. "Pierre! Are you all right?"

It was an arm! Tom could see it clearly now, and it was moving. He seemed to regain new strength at the sight of his friend's arm. A few more steps brought him parallel with the floating log. The stream was as smooth as glass and hardly seemed like the same angry, rushing, foaming water which nearly took Tom's life a short time ago.

Pierre was hurt! Tom could see the blood on his face. "Hold on, Pierre. I'm coming out to get you," called Tom to his friend. Tom, who was an excellent swimmer, dove in and started toward the injured African. Within minutes he was beside Pierre, who was still dazed from the blow on his head.

Tom took hold of the log and began to pull it toward shore. Neither boy spoke, as they knew they needed to conserve their strength as much as possible.

As Tom pulled Pierre up on the bank, he realized that he was hurt far worse than it first appeared. Besides the deep, ugly gash and swelling on his head, he also had severely cut his foot.

"Lord," prayed Tom in his heart, "please stop the bleeding and help me to know what to do."

There was no doubt about it. Pierre was badly hurt and needed medical attention as soon as possible. To leave him in the forest might mean death, as he could become prey to a lion or leopard or even a pack of wild dogs. Quickly Tom tore his shirt into strips and tied them tightly about Pierre's head and foot. He sadly thought of the first aid kit which was lost when the canoe overturned.

"This will make you feel better," said Tom to his suffering friend. "Can I get you some berries or wild fruit?"

Pierre knew what fruit would give him immediate strength, and Tom was able to find some. Pierre ate the fruit while Tom fashioned a stretcher from poles and vines.

The setting sun signaled the lateness of the hour, and darkness rapidly swept in upon them. They both thought it best to spend the night on a nearby sandbank. The warm sand felt good as they covered themselves with dry grass and leaves for protection from the cold night air.

Tom awoke somewhat refreshed, but the heat of the noonday sun seemed to drain his limited strength. The hours of pulling the heavy stretcher through the forest exhausted him completely. He did not think he could force himself to take another step, but the thought of his unconscious companion drove him on, dragging the crude stretcher behind him. Finally his body could go no farther, and he dropped to his knees.

Tom did not know how long he had been lying there when he heard a voice call, "It's Tom and Pierre." The next moments were a blur in Tom's memory as he and Pierre were carried to the nearby mission station.

The warm broth tasted good. With each swallow, Tom seemed to regain his strength. "How's Pierre?" he asked the station nurse, Edith May.

"I think he'll be all right, Tom. He's lost quite a lot of blood, but I'm able to treat him by intravenous feeding. He seems to be responding favorably." Edith was a good nurse. Her love for the people along with her medical skills had helped her gain the confidence of most of the population for miles around.

For three days the local Christians were concerned about Pierre. Tom was thrilled one morning as he paid his usual visit to his beloved friend and found him sitting up and even laughing with some of his family. Edith stopped by to chat with Pierre and went away smiling to herself.

"Thank you, Miss May," Pierre called after her. "I thank the Lord for you and the care you have given to me."

That night Bud and Mary sat in their living room talking about the boys' near tragedy when Tom entered the room. A serious look was on his face as he made his presence known.

"Dad, Mom, I have something to tell you."

Bud looked up to see Tom's eyes filled with tears. "What is it, Tom?" asked his father.

"It's about my future, Dad," answered Tom. "For a number of months I've known that the Lord wanted me to go to Bible school to prepare for His work. These last few days have confirmed the Lord's will for me." Tom paused to steady his voice. "You know how much I wanted to learn television production. Well, I want you both to know that I committed my life to the Lord just now in my room. I will be writing to your alma mater, Dad, for an application."

Our Prayer-Answering God

"... By prayer and supplication with thanksgiving let your requests be made known unto God" (Phil. 4:6).

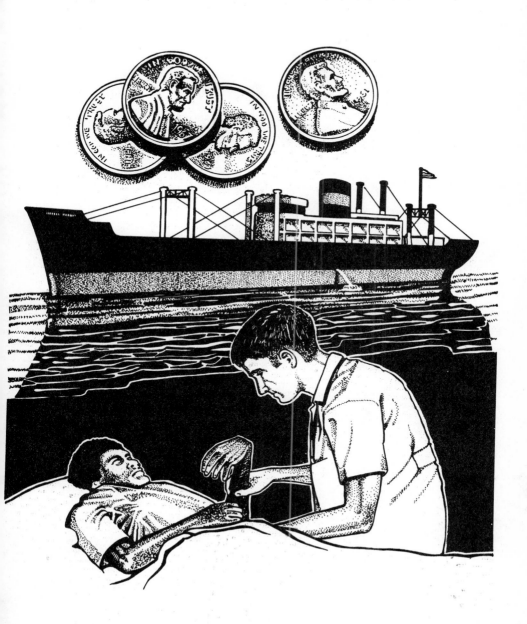

18

The Red Truck

TOM ADJUSTED THE SUN VISOR as they headed into the mainstream of the afternoon traffic. The weather was warmer than usual for February. After the recent cold spell, it seemed that the entire population of Rochester, New York, wanted to get out and enjoy the warm sunshine. Debbie was looking out the side window, watching the people as they passed by on the sidewalk. Five-year-old Pam dozed, securely strapped in the back seat.

"I sure hope this old car holds together until our furlough is over in June," said Tom as he broke the silence. "It is so rusted out, I'm afraid that one of the fenders will drop off if we hit too many holes."

Turning to her youthful looking husband, Debbie, with a twinkle in her eye, said, "Tom, we just passed a truck dealer back there. As we went by, the Lord seemed to impress upon my heart that we should inquire there regarding the purchase of a truck."

Debbie's remark came like a bolt of lightning out of the blue. They had been home from the Central African Empire for eight months, and they had been praying daily that the Lord would provide a truck for them to take back to Africa. Their first term of service convinced them that if they were to reach the distant villages, they needed a truck with which to do it.

Tom did not respond to Debbie immediately. He thought of the pickup truck brochures he had collected from various dealers. He had read each one over and over again, so that he knew exactly what he wanted in any make. Finally Tom glanced over at Debbie. "I don't want to doubt what you say, Debbie, but for some reason the Lord has not directed even one dollar to us for the purchase of a truck. We just do not have the funds. How can we ever approach a dealer to purchase a truck?" Tom had a serious look on his face.

Debbie's blue eyes seemed to speak for her as she looked at Tom. "I do believe that the Lord is saying something to us," she responded. "I know He spoke to my heart, and I think we should at least go and talk to that dealer about a truck."

Tom understood his wife too well to argue the point. He knew that Debbie would not say what she had said without being certain that the Lord directed her to say it. "God works in many wonderful ways," thought Tom. "If this is what He wants us to do, then we will follow His directions."

"I will take you and Pam home and then return to the dealer," said Tom as he turned the car into their street. Tom unbuckled their little daughter, who was fast asleep, and carried her into their apartment.

"Dear Lord, please direct Tom when he goes to see this truck dealer," prayed Debbie as they knelt together in the living room. "We want only Your will to be done."

Excitement filled Tom's heart as he parked in the parking lot. Making his way to the front of the building, he could not help but admire the row of pickup trucks to his right. "Dear Lord," he prayed softly to himself, "please help me know what to say." Inside, he admired the pictures about the showroom as well as the trucks on display.

"Can I help you, Sir?"

Tom turned to see a pleasant looking man standing beside him. "Yes, you can," answered Tom, surprising himself with his answer. "I am interested in purchasing a pickup truck."

"Do you have in mind what you want?" continued the salesman.

Tom's careful reading of the truck brochures now paid off as he told the salesman what he had in mind. "We are interested in a three-quarter ton, with a four-speed transmission, a side-mounted spare, a sun visor, a heater and larger tires than the standard size."

Tom and Debbie knew by their first-term experience that the rainy season and sandy roads called for the four-speed transmission and the extra large tires. The side-mounted spare was easier to get at and also protected the tire from the sharp rocks which they often encountered in their travels. The heater would provide warmth for the early morning chill as well as a blower to cool the cab in the heat of the day.

The salesman listened until Tom finished talking. Snapping his fingers, he motioned for Tom to follow him. "I think I have just the truck for you," he said as he pulled out a file card. "Here is a brand-new truck from last year's models. It is presently on a lot in Pennsylvania. You see, when a truck does not sell, we dealers cooperate by pooling our stock information and thus help each other sell our trucks. This is how I know about this truck. It was a special order with just the extras you requested. The farmer who ordered it refused the order, and it has been sitting on the lot since late last fall. If you want it, we will have it sent up to us."

Tom could see God working. "What is the price?" asked Tom, hardly able to control the excitement in his voice.

"Well," said the salesman, "there is a special price on it. It sells for $2100."

"What a tremendous bargain," thought Tom. "Surely this is of the Lord."

"That price can't be beat," said Tom. "I would like to discuss this with my wife. Can you put a hold on the truck for a couple of days?"

"I sure can," answered the salesman. "In fact, I will put a hold on it for three days. Will that be long enough?"

"Yes, it will," said Tom, nodding. "I am sure that you will see me by then."

Back at the apartment, Tom told Debbie what had happened.

"That's our truck," said Debbie, with tears of joy showing in her eyes. "This is the Lord's answer to our prayers."

That evening at the dinner table, Tom prayed, "Dear Father, if that is the truck You want us to have for Your work, please show us. We are asking You to lead someone to call us on the phone before this day is over and give us a gift toward the purchase of a truck. Thank You for the answer, Lord. We pray in Jesus' Name. Amen."

Debbie lifted her head and looked at Tom. "The Lord is going to answer our prayer, Tom," she said confidently.

The evening passed quickly. It was 9:30 P.M. As Tom was closing the blinds in the front room, the phone rang. "There's God's answer," shouted Tom. His hand was shaking with excitement as he picked up the phone. "Hello," he said.

"Hello, Tom. This is Dorothy, Dorothy Hill."

"How are you, Dorothy?" asked Tom.

"I'm fine, thank you," said Dorothy. "I am sorry to call you and Debbie so late at night, but I just arrived home and I felt what I have to tell you could not wait until tomorrow."

"That's all right, Dorothy," replied Tom.

"I hardly know where to begin," continued Dorothy, "but I guess it really started a number of years ago when I was in a car accident. You see, I received $1,000 from an insurance company at that time. I put it in a savings account. Since then it has earned $70 interest. Well, this morning as I was on my way to work, the Lord brought that money to mind. He laid it upon my heart to give half to Bob and Jane in the Philippines and half to you and Debbie."

"Dorothy, that's wonderful," said Tom, trying to hold back the tears.

"But there is one thing regarding your part that I feel I must tell you," Dorothy went on.

"What is it, Dorothy?" asked Tom.

"I would like you to use your funds toward the purchase of a truck," said Dorothy, not realizing that she was God's answer to Tom's prayer at the dining room table that evening.

Tom then shared with Dorothy the events that transpired that day. "I thank the Lord that He has been pleased to use me in this way," commented Dorothy just before hanging up the phone.

The next three days saw unbelievable things happen. Funds designated for the purchase of a truck came from many different sources: $5 from an eight-year-old girl; $100 from an elderly couple who had known Debbie from her childhood days; $25 from a youth group.

The third day arrived, and it was time for Tom to return to the dealer. A last-minute telephone check with the accounting department of Baptist Mid-Missions showed an even $1400 had been received for a truck. "We still need $700," Tom said to Debbie. "Maybe I should wait for today's mail before I go."

The mailman came but left only a few advertisements. In Debbie's prayer before Tom left the house, she said, "Lord, we believe that this truck is the one You have for us. Somehow in Your own perfect way, supply the needed $700 for us today."

Tom arrived at the garage. Instead of parking in the back parking lot, he parked on the street in front of the showroom windows.

"Well, I see you are back," remarked the salesman with a big smile.

"That's right," said Tom, wondering just what the Lord was going to do. "We definitely want that truck, but we only have $1400 on hand."

The salesman looked at Tom. "What are you driving now?"

Tom motioned to the secondhand, rust-eaten car sitting at the curb in front of the garage. "There she is right there," he answered.

The salesman walked over to the window, stuck his hands in his pockets and seemed to be studying the old car.

"Surely he is not interested in that old thing," thought Tom.

"I'll tell you what I will do," said the salesman as he turned to Tom. "You give me the $1400 and your car, and you can have the truck."

"That's a deal," replied Tom immediately, surprising himself with such a fast answer.

Two days later Tom, Debbie and Pam were traveling in their new truck to prayer meeting. "Red truck," said Debbie as she patted the dash with her hand, "the Lord gave you to us, and He is going to use you in Africa to take the gospel to those who have never heard. Thank You, Lord," she said softly, wiping away a tear.

"Thank You, Jesus," whispered Pam, sitting between them.

19

God's Four-Cent Surplus

GEORGE STEPPED FROM THE PHONE BOOTH into the blowing snow. A troubled look spread across his face as he headed toward his car, which to him was like a home away from home in his deputation travels. He opened the car door and slipped into the front seat. He welcomed the warm air from the heater after standing fifteen minutes in the cold phone booth trying to complete his call to Nan. They had been home from the Central African Empire for seven months, but they still were not accustomed to the cold weather.

The talk with Nan was no comfort. "I was up all night with Kathy," she said. "Her head cold settled in her chest. Her temperature is still 103°. I'm not asking you to come home, George, but I did want to tell you of Kathy's condition."

This winter had been very hard on the Erickson family. Both George and Nan had had a bout with the flu, and then Billy. Seven-year-old Kathy seemed to have it the worst of all. George called every day and sometimes twice a day, but he felt so helpless. Then, too, there was the matter of finances. In the past two weeks George had been in three churches which might provide future support. But he had an immediate need for funds. He had $2.85; and he was sure that Nan didn't have more than that—if as much.

The longer he thought about it, the more he desired to return home to Nan and the children. He had two gas company credit cards; so that would help him get home without using any of his cash. His next meeting was Sunday, and this was Thursday morning. Then, too, Sunday's meeting was two hundred miles closer to home! He bowed his head and committed the situation to the Lord. "Father," he prayed, "my family needs me right now. Kathy is sick. We're almost completely out of funds. Please help us, Lord. Show me what You would have me do."

He returned to the phone booth. "Hello, Nan . . ." began George.

Before she hung up, Nan cautioned: "Do be careful. The weather bureau predicts ten inches of snow before tomorrow."

At seven o'clock that evening, George drove into his driveway. "Thank You, Lord, for bringing me safely home," he sighed as he unbuckled his seat belt and opened the car door. He was met at the back door by Nan. Three-year-old Billy was dressed in his pajamas but was too excited to sleep. Daddy was coming!

"How's Kathy?" George asked Nan.

"Well, she seems to be some better. Her temperature has dropped to 100°, but she has developed a terrible cough!"

George walked into the children's bedroom. "Hi, Sweetheart," he smiled. "Daddy's come home to see how his little girl is coming along." He bent down and kissed Kathy on her forehead and squeezed her shoulder.

"I'm glad you're home, Daddy. I missed you," said the little girl. George turned his head away and wiped his eyes.

"Well, Daddy's home, Honey. Now get better so we can play. OK?" he said as he winked at her.

Even though the fever lessened, Kathy coughed hard all night long. "We have to call a doctor," George told Nan shortly before sunrise.

"I know we do," she said with a question in her voice, "but we must have money enough to pay him."

"How much do you have?"

"I don't have much. Only $1.99. The Lord sent you home at the right time."

George hesitated before summing up their situation: "I have just $2.85, which makes a total of $4.84. Two churches will be sending money in the mail. The Lord knows all about it. He will not fail."

Nan got out of bed and hurried to Kathy's room as she began violently coughing. "Help me, Mommy. Oh, help me," the small girl called to her mother. George slipped out of bed to his knees and began to pray.

Breakfast was over. During devotions Kathy began to cough again. Nan went to her room. When she came back, the color had drained from her face.

"What's wrong, Honey?" asked George.

Nan answered in a whisper, "Kathy is bleeding internally. She just vomited blood."

George was sick. "Is she bleeding badly?"

"I don't know. I do know something's not right."

As Nan disappeared into the bedroom, George picked up the phone book. "I'm calling a doctor." He felt as drained as Nan looked. "Lord, direct me," he prayed, as he examined the list of physicians. His finger ran down the page and then stopped. "Dr. Woods," he said to himself and dialed the number.

A nurse answered, and George asked if he could speak to the doctor. Immediately, the doctor was on the line. George explained: "This is George Erickson. I have a seven-year-old daughter who is sick with a chest infection. She just vomited blood."

"Has she been coughing a lot?"

"Yes, Doctor. She started coughing yesterday afternoon. She coughed all night."

"What's your address?" George gave it. With a quick, "I'll be right over!" Dr. Woods hung up.

George could hardly believe it, especially since Dr. Woods' office was on the opposite side of the city. He shared this with Nan, who was sitting beside Kathy's bed.

"How did you know whom to call?" she asked George.

"I didn't know, but the Lord knew. He stopped my finger at just the right name."

Dr. Woods was a man about fifty years old. He was soft-spoken and had a very kind face. He examined Kathy. Looking into her pretty face, he said, "You'll be all right, Honey. I'm going to order some good medicine for you." He patted Kathy on the side of her face.

In the front room, he told George that the blood came from a ruptured blood vessel in Kathy's throat. "I'll give you a prescription for an antibiotic and cough medicine. That should take care of her." He wrote out the prescriptions.

George wanted to ask him if he could pay him some other time for the visit, but he couldn't gather the courage to do so.

"Here you are, Mr. Erickson." Dr. Woods handed George the prescriptions. "As for my visit today, that's on me."

George couldn't believe his ears. The Lord had sent them a stranger, but one who had offered his services free. The doctor headed for the door, shook George's hand and called good-bye to Nan and Kathy.

When the door closed, George bowed his head to thank God for this miracle. Nan walked into the front room with her eyes filled with tears. "George," she said, "God just did a miracle for us."

George held up the two prescriptions. "What shall I do with these?"

Nan's eyes met his. "If the Lord can direct your finger to the right name in the phone book, He can keep the price of those prescriptions below $4.84. We'll trust Him for that, Hon."

George was already slipping on his coat to go to the corner drugstore. Walking through the snow, George prayed all the way: "Father, don't let this cost more than I have in my pocket." He knew Nan was praying too.

In the store he handed the prescriptions to the pharmacist, who retreated to his bottles and jars. George reached into his pocket, counted the money and replaced it. It was still $4.84. "I ask, dear Father," he repeated, "to keep the charge for these prescriptions from going over the amount I have in my pocket." He returned to the pharmacy counter. "Sir," he called, "could you please tell me how much these prescriptions will be?"

The pharmacist took a pencil and began to figure. "Yes, I can," he answered; "that will be $4.80."

20

The Day the Engines Quit

"DADDY, I DON'T HEAR the motor running."
Seven-year-old Penny raised herself high enough to peer over
the top of the side board of her lower bunk.

Tom Kane stirred from a sound sleep. "Did you say
something, Penny?"

"I don't hear the ship's motor, Daddy. When I woke up, I
didn't hear it making its noise."

Tom realized that the vibrations of the ship's diesel had
stopped. For five days he had tried to get accustomed to the
constant vibration, accompanied by the distant rumble which
came from the heart of the great steel vessel. Now it was silent,
and he knew it was neither the time nor the place for it to be idle.

"What do you think is wrong, Tom?" inquired Jane from the
bunk below.

"I don't know," answered Tom as he looked at his watch.
"It's three o'clock, and it won't be daylight for another three
hours."

The Kanes had chosen the freighter *Loudima* because they
had heard how comfortable and interesting it was to travel on a
large cargo ship. They had choice accommodations: a three-room
suite, a beautiful lounge and meals with the captain at his private
dining table. The first five days of ocean travel were filled with
excitement as they did everything from watching porpoises to
having picnics on the sun deck.

"Well, there's nothing we can do about it, so we might as
well go back to sleep." Tom crawled down from his bunk and

looked out the cabin window. "It sure is a beautiful night out there. The moonlight on the ocean looks like a shining highway."

"Daddy, let me see too," requested Penny as she tumbled out of bed and ran to the window. Tom lifted her to the porthole.

"All right, Penny, back to bed now. We have a big day planned tomorrow."

The brightness of the morning sun awakened Tom. He glanced at his watch. "Eight o'clock," he whispered to himself. "We have really overslept." He quietly descended from his upper bunk and looked out the window. The ocean was as smooth as a tabletop, and Tom could see that the ship was standing still. It was a strange feeling to sit like a floating duck in the middle of the Atlantic Ocean. Several workmen could be seen chipping paint from the railing below.

"The captain is sorry that he can't eat with you this morning, but he is below in the engine room," said Stanley, the English steward who was standing at the dining room entrance. A serving towel was draped over one arm.

"What seems to be the trouble, Stanley?" asked Tom as he entered the room behind Jane and Penny.

"Our diesel broke down about midnight, and the auxiliary engine has also developed some minor problems. The captain says that we should be on our way by noon."

"Does this happen very often, Stanley?" asked Jane.

"No, it doesn't. In fact, I have been on the seas for fifteen years, and this is the first time I have seen such a thing."

Stanley stood with bowed head as Penny and then Tom thanked the Lord for their food. He smiled as he caught Penny glancing at him when she lifted her head. "If you don't mind my saying so, Mr. Kane, I think it's jolly nice of you to pray before you eat. We used to do it at home when I was a boy."

The comment from the steward surprised Tom and Jane. For several days Tom had been seeking the opportunity to witness to Stanley.

"Thank you, Stanley. We always make it a practice to thank the Lord for our food."

"I know it will please you, Sir, to hear that the captain appreciates your praying at his table. He's not a very religious man, but he says something is different and real about you people from the ordinary religious people he has seen."

"We appreciate those kind remarks, Stanley. Thank you for

sharing them with us."

Tom's heart leaped within him. Little did he realize the impression their family was making on the crew of the *Loudima*.

"It's just one of those things that may happen once in a sailor's lifetime, Mr. Kane." Captain Swank had made his way up to the sun deck to talk with the missionary family.

"What happened, Captain Swank?" asked Jane, squinting her eyes as she looked up from the deck chair.

The captain hesitated a moment, searching for descriptive terms which Jane would understand. He didn't know she had taken a mechanics course in her Bible school missions training. "A connecting rod broke in the main engine. When we went to start the auxiliary engine, we found a few minor problems there as well. Since the ocean is so calm, I decided to do all the repairs this morning. Now we have two engines as good as new."

"Has this ever happened to you before, Captain?" asked Tom.

"No, this is a new experience for me. I must say, it is most unusual."

The ship's motor rumbled into action, and the vibrations once again were transmitted throughout the steel structure.

Penny ran excitedly to her parents. "Mommy, Daddy, it's moving! The ship's moving!"

"You're right, Penny," said the captain. "We're on our way to the Canary Islands."

"I prayed last night that Jesus would help you fix the ship," said Penny as she walked over to the captain and held his hand. "I'm glad Jesus helped you."

The middle-aged sea captain was at a loss for words. Never had anyone talked to him that way about Christ. Captain Swank picked her up in his arms and smiled. "Thank you, Penny. It looks like He answered your prayers."

"He always answers my prayers. He loves me." There was silence and then she spoke again. "Jesus loves you too, Captain. He died for us on the cross."

The captain hugged her and placed her on the deck. Tom and Jane knew that his heart was touched. He tried to speak and then turned to look at the ocean, fighting to keep back the tears.

"Penny is right, Captain Swank," said Tom as he stood up and walked over beside the captain. "God loves you and sent His Son, Jesus Christ, to die for your sins." He noticed the captain's eyes were wet with tears.

"I know what Penny was talking about, Mr. Kane. I had a mother who was a wonderful Christian woman. She took me to Sunday school and church when I was a boy. When I was eleven years old, she died and left three children orphans. You see, my father died when I was a baby. Since the time my mother died, I've not been in contact with those boyhood teachings."

"Let me ask you, Captain Swank. Have you ever accepted Jesus Christ as your Savior?"

"No, I haven't, Mr. Kane. I thought about it as a boy, but I never made the decision."

"Jesus died to pay the penalty for your sins. He can give you eternal life right here and now if you will accept Him. Will you do it, Captain?"

"Yes, Mr. Kane, I will." The captain and Tom bowed their heads as the veteran sea captain prayed that God would save him. The captain turned to Tom after he finished praying. "That Penny is something else. She sure knows how to reach a guy's heart."

"All I can say, Captain, is that the Lord used her today."

"Yes, He did. And you know something else, Mr. Kane?"

"What's that, Captain?"

"I'm glad both of our engines broke down."

The two men laughed and turned to go back to Jane and Penny.

21

An Unseen Hand

THE SPEEDY MOTORBIKE seemed to know its way through the crowded Paris streets. The large clock at the St. Lazare railroad station showed the early morning commuters that it was 7:33 A.M. Winding his way unnoticed through the heavy traffic was Don Gibson, the young missionary who was on his way to the Alliance Francaise where he was studying the French language.

"I wish I didn't have to learn French," said Don to himself as he dodged between two small cars. He remembered so well the difficult time he had with language in high school. But learning French was required by the mission before he and Shirley could go to the Chad Republic.

He loved the crowded streets with little cars darting here and there and horns blaring on every side. "This is Paris," he thought. "Just like I read about in the books back home in America." And now he was actually seeing it and being a part of the busy life of the famous city. Such thoughts would make most anyone excited and help him forget his problems. After all, this was a once-in-a-lifetime experience.

Don and Shirley had arrived in France six months before. As he rode along, he recalled how God had provided a three-room apartment for them when apartments were so scarce. He mustered a little smile as he thought of his expertise in sign language those first few months, especially with the shop merchants on their street who had adopted this American family as their own. He remembered how the Lord had provided the motorbike for his transportation. The basket seat fastened to the back of the bike told him of the Lord's blessings in bringing Ann into their lives. The accumulation of thoughts touched Don's heart and brought tears to his eyes. "Thank You, Lord, for Your many blessings," he prayed above the drone of the bike's motor.

Then he thought of Shirley's last words to him that morning as she had kissed him good-bye. "Don't worry, Don. The Lord will provide for us." He could visualize her sweet smiling face as she spoke to him. Shirley was referring to the fact that unexpected expenses that month had wiped out their financial reserves. They had eaten the last of their food that morning, and they still had one more week before their support check was due from their mission's headquarters in Cleveland, Ohio.

Don breathed a prayer. "Please, Father, supply us with the food we need. Make it possible for us to have our noon meal today."

Try as he would, Don couldn't concentrate on his classroom studies. Shirley's last words seemed to echo back and forth in his mind. "Don't worry, Don. The Lord will provide for us."

Before he realized it, the class was over for the day, and he was once again threading his way through the congested traffic. "Lord," he prayed, "I know You are going to supply our need somehow. We are here because You placed us here, and we are trusting You to undertake for us." Then he thought about the day's mail. This would be the logical way for the Lord to answer their prayers and send them the needed funds. Excitement began to build as he pictured himself opening an envelope and finding God's answer.

No sooner had he pulled over to the curb at their apartment building then the mailman appeared. Pushing his motorbike into the inner court, Don followed the familiar blue uniform. He lifted the bike to its stand and locked it.

"Hi, Daddy," called a little voice. Don looked up and saw Shirley and Ann looking through the protective bars surrounding their fifth-floor balcony. Ann's small hand was waving through the bars.

"Hi, up there," called Don. "I'll be right up as soon as I get the mail."

The mailman gave a handful of letters to the waiting landlady, who quickly looked through them. "I'm sorry, Mr. Gibson." The kind face looked up at Don. "I have nothing for you today."

The young missionary couldn't hide his disappointment. He couldn't believe what he had heard. "Now what will we do?" Don thought to himself. "I thought for sure this was the way that God would answer our prayers."

He turned to start up the steps. "Thank you, Madame," he said to the smiling landlady. He looked at his watch. His heart seemed to skip a beat as he saw that it was already 11:15 A.M. "Lord," he prayed silently as he mounted the stairs, "the shops close at noon and won't open again until 2:00 P.M. Time is running out on us. Please, Lord, help us. Shirley and I can do without food for a while but not our little Ann, Lord."

Shirley was standing with Ann in the open kitchen door as Don reached the fifth-floor level. "There's no mail, Honey," he said with a touch of disappointment in his voice. He picked up Ann in his arms and hugged her.

"That's all right," responded Shirley. "The Lord is not limited to our ways. He doesn't have to follow our plans to supply our needs."

Don glanced at his watch. "Only thirty-seven minutes left until the stores close," he thought to himself. "Shirley," said Don with new confidence filling his voice, "let's commit our need to the Lord again. It will take a miracle to put food on our table for noon, and I believe that we should ask the Lord for that miracle."

The two young missionaries and their little daughter knelt in prayer beside a small sofa which was in their combination living-dining room. As Shirley was praying, Don heard a sound in the hall. Since there were two apartments on that level, he thought perhaps it was the people next door. It seemed strange to him not to hear a door open or close. He heard the noise again, and it seemed to be at their door. Looking over his shoulder, he saw an envelope being slipped under the door. Shirley, unaware of what was happening, prayed at that moment, "Thank You, Lord, for the wonderful way You are going to answer our prayers today. In Jesus' Name I pray, Amen."

Don got up from his knees, walked to the door and picked up the envelope. Opening it, he found several franc bills worth about $1.75. Kneeling beside Shirley, he laid the bills on the sofa.

"Oh, Don," sobbed Shirley, "God has answered our prayers. He has directed this money to us!" Once again the family thanked the Lord for supplying their needs.

"Hey!" said Don looking at his watch, "it's 11:40. If we're going to have our noon meal, I'd better get going." As he started down the steps, he could hear Ann singing to her mother, "Jesus loves me, this I know. For the Bible tells me so."

That night Don read the Bible account of the feeding of the five thousand. "Isn't it wonderful," said Shirley, "that God loves us and cares for us too? Just as He provided food for all those people, so did He for us today."

Don smiled. "That's right; even if He did send it by an unseen hand."

22

God's Perfect Timing

"WHAT ARE YOUR PLANS for tomorrow, Randy?" asked Jan as she came from the bedroom after tucking in Andy for the night.

"Oh, it's time to make out the payroll for the workmen again," answered Randy, snapping shut his loose-leaf notebook. "But before I get into that, I want to finish these last two Bible lessons on the Book of Mark."

This was the second term of missionary service for Randy and Jan Allen. Their first term had been spent in the Republic of Chad, but during their first furlough a personnel need developed in the Central African Empire. Believing that God was leading them, they had gone to that landlocked country in the heart of Africa. Two years after their return to Africa, the Lord blessed their home with Andrew, who received the nickname Andy.

The Lord had greatly blessed the ministry of the Allens at Ippy, the station which had the largest Baptist Mid-Missions' medical work. Since their return to Africa, they had the joy of visiting on a regular basis all of the pastors in their district. Besides the progress made in the outstation and village ministry, the mission station itself was taking on a new look as construction and remodeling took place. One of Randy's satisfactory achievements was the construction of a new church building seating 500 people.

"Are you ready to turn in for the night, Jan?" asked Randy of his faithful companion.

"All right with me," she responded, rubbing her eyes.

Randy hadn't realized just how tired he was, and sleep quickly claimed him.

With the early morning routine over, Randy began the tedious job of the work payroll. He and Jan were up at five o'clock as usual and seemed to have everything pretty well under control. Randy had devotions in the chapel with his workmen and then hurried home to have breakfast with Jan and a missionary family who stopped overnight on their way to Bambari to buy supplies. He usually could count on several hours of work to get the payroll slips ready to pay the workmen.

Halfway through the morning, Jan brought in some iced tea and cookies, which really hit the spot. "If I can only get everything done by noon," thought Randy, "I can pay the workmen before they return to the village for their two-hour siesta break." Time was essential for Randy as he worked on the papers.

With his thoughts focused on his paperwork, Randy suddenly felt that the Holy Spirit was speaking to him. In fact, he was so sure that God was speaking, it couldn't have been any clearer had he read the message on the paper before him or heard an audible voice. He stopped what he was doing and bowed his head. Quietly he whispered, "Speak, Lord, for I am listening."

The young missionary sat motionless, waiting upon the Lord. In the short time that followed, the Lord impressed upon Randy's heart to count out 500 francs (about $2) and give them to Pastor Luke, the station church pastor.

Randy reached into his right hip pocket and pulled out some 100-franc bills. Carefully he counted out the amount the Lord had told him. He placed the remaining bills into his right pocket and the roll of 500 francs in his left pocket. As he did so, he said softly, "I don't understand it all, Lord, but whatever You want me to do, I want to do it."

He called to his African houseboy: "John, run down to Pastor Luke's house and tell him that I would like to see him just as soon as possible."

By this time Randy was thrilled with excitement. God was doing something and was pleased to use him in whatever it was. In fifteen minutes John returned and told him that the pastor was waiting for him. "Thank You, Lord," whispered Randy as he left his office to meet Pastor Luke, his African co-worker and brother in Christ.

Randy seemed lost for words, but he finally spoke to Pastor

Luke. "Pastor," said Randy excitedly, "the Lord told me to do this." He stepped forward, reached into his left pocket for the roll of bills and dropped them into Pastor Luke's outstretched hands.

When he saw the money in his hands, Pastor Luke dropped his head and began to cry. Randy was so deeply touched he, too, began to weep. Finally gaining control of himself, Pastor Luke looked at Randy. "Sir," he said through the sobs, "the Lord did this. He has worked through you to bring about this miraculous answer to prayer."

Pastor Luke proceeded to tell Randy how that morning after his children had eaten and left for school, his wife, Ann, had told him that their food supply was completely gone. "In fact," she said, "we don't even have anything in our garden which is ready to eat." They had then prayed together before she left to work in the garden.

"You see, Sir," said Pastor Luke, "I could go begging in the village, and any number of people would give us food. But, Sir, I don't believe the Lord would have me do that. After my wife left for the garden, I went out behind our house and slipped off into the tall elephant grass where no one could see or hear me. It was there I fell on my knees before God and praised Him for His faithfulness. I told him of our need for food and claimed His promises for us. What wonderful, blessed fellowship I had with Him, Sir." Pastor Luke wiped his eyes as he talked.

"When I had finished praying, I got on my feet just praising the Lord for Himself and for what He was going to do for us. I felt that the Lord was in full control and He would work out everything. I made my way out of the grass and found your houseboy, John, looking for me. He told me you wanted to see me, and I came directly to your house."

Randy could picture it all. God had spoken to him at the same time Pastor Luke was on his knees pouring his heart out to the Lord in prayer. It all fit together perfectly. "Yes, go on," said Randy, with a heart bursting with joy.

"Well, Sir," answered Pastor Luke, "that's all there is to it. I simply came in answer to your request, and upon my arrival you gave me this money." Pastor Luke continued, "I want to take this opportunity to thank God for supplying our need, and I want to thank you for being in that place of communion with Him where He could speak to you and you could hear Him."

Randy and Pastor Luke shook hands, and the African pastor started back to the village. Randy watched him until he disappeared over the hill. Before returning to the house, he quietly prayed, "Father, thank You for this blessed experience. Thank You for men like Pastor Luke and the privilege of knowing him. Thank You for Your faithfulness and for the opportunity of being used by You today."

Randy returned to his desk of papers. He thought about the work yet to be done on them, and picked up his pen. But before doing so, he bowed his head and prayed, "Dear Lord, thank You for that interruption today. Help me to remember that Your timing is always perfect and Your ways are always best."

23

The Chief's Decision

FRANK BYMERS ROLLED RESTLESSLY on his bed. Glancing at his illuminated watch, he saw that it was four o'clock. The first light of day would soon be making its way into the little mission house located at the medical station of Ippy in the Central African Empire. He couldn't keep from thinking about the canton chief at Yambo, a large village of 200 homes, forty miles into the bush.

Just the day before Frank had received an urgent message from Joshua Mamba, the village pastor, to come immediately. The chief's fifteen-year-old daughter had fallen on a rock and cut an artery in her leg.

Frank and June had left right away for Yambo. As their pickup truck entered the village, men and women everywhere in the village were crying the death wail. Pastor Joshua ran up to the truck with a worried look on his face.

"Mr. Bymers, she may be already dead. She has lost a lot of blood. The chief tells me that if she dies, he is going to force me out of the village and close the church. He says my God was not powerful enough to protect his daughter."

Frank knew that the chief would carry out his threat if his daughter died. Quickly he ran to the chief's hut and knelt beside the girl. He gently opened her eyelid and noticed the whiteness of the flesh inside the eye. "She's lost a lot of blood," he murmured. He couldn't feel any heartbeat, but he knew she was still alive.

"Chief," he said in a clear, distinct voice, "come with me. I need to take your daughter to the mission station."

Even in the dim light of the small kerosene lamp, Frank could see the glare of the chief's bloodshot eyes. "You want to kill her. That's what you want to do. But since she is dead already, or nearly dead, I'm going to force you to take her with you! If she doesn't come back to this village alive, you and your preacher boy are finished in my district."

"Dear Lord," Frank prayed silently, "spare this girl. Keep this village open to the gospel and save this canton chief."

The almost lifeless form of the young girl was placed on a mattress in the back of the truck. The chief and three of his wives got in with her. Frank drove as fast as he could safely go on the treacherous road. June prayed silently beside the young girl in the back of the truck.

As he drove Frank prayed that Dr. Sims would be home from Bambari, where he had gone to have repair work done on his truck. The girl needed a blood transfusion. But to the Banda tribe the transfer of blood from one body to another was a white man's curse. It meant death or sickness to both people.

Turning down the hospital drive, Frank saw the doctor's truck. He breathed a prayer of thanks to the Lord.

"She's just about dead, Frank," said Dr. Sims. "Only a miracle by the Lord will save this girl."

One of Dr. Sim's African assistants was busy in the lab finding out the girl's blood type. "It's O-positive, Doctor," the young assistant said as he rushed into the operating room.

Frank's heart beat with excitement. "Ed, that's my type. Take my blood for the girl," said Frank as he unbuttoned his shirt.

The canton chief had never been in a hospital before. He stood in amazement, looking at the spotless room with all of its equipment. His eyes widened as the white missionary's arm was punctured by an African assistant. The chief could hardly believe that a white man would give his blood, especially for an African he didn't know.

Dr. Sims loosened the tourniquet which Pastor Joshua had so expertly put on the girl's leg. "Praise the Lord, Fran," Dr. Sims said to the missionary nurse. "I believe the girl is going to make it. We'll be able to tell better tomorrow morning. I want you to stay with her tonight if you will."

Fran knew the seriousness of the case and nodded her approval to her missionary co-worker.

After the evening meal that night in the Bymers' home, Frank and June and their two sons prayed for the chief's daughter.

"Dear Lord," ten-year-old Stephen prayed, "please don't let this girl die. Help her to get well. I pray that she and her father and others in her family will accept Jesus as their Savior."

As Frank lay in his bed that night, he could hear the chief's voice over and over again telling him that if his daughter died there would be no more preaching the gospel in his entire district.

The next morning Frank walked into the hospital. He was relieved to see that the young girl was awake and alert. Fran, who looked worn out from her sleepless night, had fastened a pole alongside the hospital cot for the intravenous feeding and blood transfusion.

"This is the white man I told you about," the chief said to his daughter. "You now have his blood in your body." He quickly added, "And don't you worry, my daughter, for you're going to get well."

Frank could hardly believe his ears. The chief's attitude had changed overnight. The chief got up from the girl's side and motioned for Frank to follow him.

Once outside the hospital, he turned to Frank. "Mr. Bymers, forgive me for what I said to you last night. I can see that you missionaries love us and show your love in many ways. You did what I wouldn't do. You gave your blood to save my daughter's life."

Tears came to the chief's eyes. Frank reached out and patted him on the shoulder.

"Chief," he said in a low, serious voice, "I'm glad to do what I did. I would do it again if I had the opportunity. But let me tell you about One who gave all of His blood for you and for me."

The chief listened intently as Frank clearly explained the wonderful gospel story. God manifested His love through the death of His Son, Jesus Christ, on the cross of Calvary. "My blood, Chief, can only extend your daughter's physical life; but the blood of Jesus Christ can give her eternal life."

The chief, realizing his lost condition and what Christ had done for him, looked squarely into Frank's eyes. "Mr. Bymers, can I have everlasting life?"

What a thrill it was to the young missionary to lead the canton chief to Christ there in the hospital yard.

Returning to the hospital room, the chief excitedly told his daughter that he had received Christ as his Savior.

The young girl looked up from her cot: "I want Jesus as my Savior, too, Father."

"Mr. Bymers," said the girl's father, "please help my daughter as you helped me."

Frank and the canton chief knelt beside the cot as the young girl prayed for Christ to become her Savior.

"This week has been the best in all my life," said the canton chief to Pastor Joshua. He had bicycled forty miles to the hospital to see his village friends.

The pastor's face was beaming with joy because of the salvation of the chief and his daughter. He believed great blessings were in store for the village of Yambo.

24

Trapped!

"DID YOU HEAR THAT NDOLI is missing?" Harold asked as he came into the house.

Wilma looked up from the sofa where she was darning socks. "No, I haven't heard. How long has he been gone?"

"Well, Chief Kolo told me this noon that he has been missing for two days now."

Wilma stopped her darning. "Do they have any idea what happened to him?"

"Yes, they do," said Harold, "but I don't even like to think of it. Some of the older folks believe that he was caught by a leopard or lion."

"What a terrible thought," gasped Wilma.

Someone clapped their hands in the backyard.

"It's Chief Kolo from Boali," said Wilma. "He's standing in the driveway with a group of men."

Harold went to the backyard to greet the chief.

"Mr. Acker," spoke Chief Kolo, "I've come to ask you to take us to the river in your pickup. I don't think Ndoli would go any farther than that. If he is alive, we need to get to him soon. Your answer could mean life or death for Ndoli, Mr. Acker."

Harold felt like he was in the spotlight as the men waited for his answer. The young missionary couple knew Ndoli well. Ever since his parents moved to Boali, Ndoli was a source of trouble. He stole from gardens, broke into homes, and even speared holes in the aluminum roof of the mission dispensary. Every time Harold or Wilma tried to talk with him about the Lord, he would ignore them and walk away.

Harold looked at the chief. "All right, Chief; I'll take you. Since we no doubt will spend the night in the forest, I need a little time to pack some things."

"I don't know how long we'll be out there," Harold said to Wilma, "but this could be a wonderful opportunity to reach the chief and his men with the gospel." He hesitated before continuing: "And if we do find Ndoli alive, maybe I'll be able to witness to him too."

After about an hour's travel, they reached the river. "Well, here we are, Chief," said the young missionary.

"Mr. Acker, I know that you have a powerful God! Do you think He can help if you call on Him?"

"I know He can," answered Harold.

"Then I'm calling my men together before they begin the search. I want you to pray for all of us." Without any further word, Chief Kolo called out a command. The men obediently gathered in a circle near the truck.

As Harold prayed, he thanked God for His love for them and for sending His Son to die that they might live. He asked God to direct them to Ndoli.

"Thank you, Mr. Acker," said the chief. "We appreciate your prayer for us."

Within minutes the men received their instructions and disappeared among the trees. The missionary and the chief remained by the truck.

"Chief," Harold began, "I don't know the jungle like you do, but maybe you and I could go in that direction."

"That's fine with me, Mr. Acker," answered the chief. "It will soon be dark, and I don't want you to be away from your truck in the darkness."

The two men started into the heavy undergrowth. As they walked, Harold prayed that somehow God would help them locate Ndoli.

"Did you hear that?" asked the chief, cupping his hand to his ear.

"Hear what?" asked Harold, stopping to listen.

Both men stood in silence.

"There it is again," said the chief, "and it's coming from that direction over there."

Harold did hear a faint sound. "Yes, I heard it, Chief. It is coming from that direction."

After a few minutes they heard it again. It was a voice. It was somewhat muffled, but someone was definitely calling for help.

"It's Ndoli's voice," said the chief with excitement. "It's Ndoli, and he's in that clump of bushes."

Pushing closer, the two men found that Ndoli had fallen into an abandoned trap. "Ndoli," called Chief Kolo, "are you all right?"

"I think my leg is broken," answered Ndoli. "I can't move it."

Harold crawled to the mouth of the hole and looked in. As his eyes adjusted to the dark hole, he made out the figure of Ndoli lying on the bottom, some fifteen feet down. "Don't worry, Ndoli," Harold called. "We'll have you out in a short time."

Chief Kolo gave a long, loud, high call—the signal to the men that Ndoli was found and their help was needed.

"I'll go down to Ndoli, Chief," Harold said. "Maybe I can put splints on his leg while the men are coming."

The chief cut some vines and wrapped them around a nearby tree. He tied one end to Harold's waist and, bracing his feet against the tree, lowered the missionary into the dark hole.

"Mr. Acker," said Ndoli, "I'm glad to see you. I thought I would die in here."

"The Lord directed us to you, Ndoli," said Harold. "We'll have plenty of time to talk after I look at that leg of yours."

In the dim light, it looked like Ndoli's leg was broken just above the ankle. It was swollen badly and very tender to touch.

"Chief," called Harold, "go to my truck and bring me the white box behind the seat. I also need two of those short boards in the back of the truck. Oh, yes, bring my food box and that canteen of water on the front seat."

"There you are, Ndoli," said Harold as he finished tying the splints on his leg. "How did that sandwich taste?"

"I'll never be able to repay you for what you have done for me, Mr. Acker," said Ndoli.

"Well, I'll tell you, Ndoli," said Harold, "the best way you can repay me is by accepting Jesus as your Savior. I don't have to tell you that He died for you. You have heard that in church many times."

Darkness now covered the jungle. A lion's roar could be heard now and then in the distance. A hyena howled nearby. The last of the men arrived at the trap.

"Mr. Acker," asked Ndoli, "I know this is an unusual time

and place for this request, but would it be possible for me to accept Jesus right now?"

"This is a wonderful time and place, Ndoli," said Harold.

The two men bowed their heads as Ndoli asked Christ to forgive him of his sins and to save him.

"What about us up here, Mr. Acker?" asked Chief Kolo.

At Harold's invitation, the chief and six of his men accepted Christ as their Savior.

"What a wonderful answer to prayer," Harold thought to himself.

Ndoli was carefully pulled from the hole and carried to the truck. The trip back to the mission station was slow but a blessed one for the men. They were filled with excitement. They had found Ndoli, and they had new life in Christ.

Later that night Harold and Wilma transported Ndoli to a nearby government hospital. "Just think of it," said Harold, "Ndoli accepted Christ down in that hole."

"That's right," said Wilma. "Ndoli was trapped so he could live."

25

Chain of Miracles

RUTH PRATT LOOKED UP from the kitchen sink where she was washing the supper dishes. "What is it, Don?"

Her husband looked worried as he read the official government paper in his hand. "I can't understand it, Ruth. Our visa request was rejected. We must leave the country by six o'clock tomorrow night."

"Six o'clock tomorrow night!" gasped Ruth, grabbing a towel to dry her hands. "Why that means we will have to start tonight in order to get to the border on time."

They had just twenty-three hours to get to the border, nine hundred miles away. With the roads in such bad condition, it would take a miracle to get there in time. "I'll get the suitcases!" shouted Don on his way out the back door to the small shed behind the house.

Ruth's heart ached as she looked around the mission house, their home for the past eight years. "I wish we had time to pack a couple of barrels," she whispered to herself.

Within minutes Don was back with two large suitcases. "I'll help you, Honey. We should be on the road in thirty minutes."

In just a short time the suitcases were packed, closed and carried to the car. "I hope we make it with this thing," said Don, shaking his head. "I've had trouble lately with the battery and tires."

Ruth made a last-minute check through the house. Don ran over to the national pastor's house to tell him of the recent development. David Kim was heartbroken when he heard the news. "But, Mr. Pratt," said David holding Don's hand, "this is so sudden. When did you receive the official notice?"

"Just about an hour ago, David. A runner brought it from the post."

The veteran pastor walked with his beloved missionary to the waiting car. Ruth held four-year-old Tommy on her lap. "Good-bye, Mrs. Pratt. God bless you. We will be praying for you, and we hope you can come back to us."

David seemed to know that his missionary friends would not return. Too many missionaries had their visas rejected these days and didn't return. David prayed and then hugged Don and Ruth.

The long hours of the night seemed like an endless nightmare. Ruth tried her best to stay awake to keep Don company while he drove. Young Tommy found a comfortable spot on his mother's lap and slept soundly.

"What time is it?" yawned Ruth. She opened her eyes and saw the red glow in the eastern sky. "I must have gone to sleep."

"It's six o'clock," answered Don. The fatigue began to show in his face. "I'll stop to fill the gas tank in the next town, and maybe we can get some breakfast."

The town was a typical little settlement. Very few people were on the streets at that early hour. Don found the only gas pump in town and knocked on the door of the storekeeper's house to awaken him. The clerk wasn't too happy to get up, but he managed to throw on his robe and come outside. While the precious liquid was pumped into the almost empty tank, the Pratts ate a quick meal. Don paid for the gas, and they were soon on their way.

A loud, hissing noise was heard over the roar of the motor. Don knew it was tire trouble as the steering became difficult. The car came to a halt. "Oh, no," groaned Don, looking at the tire. "It's a flat tire. A rock cut through one of the front tires, and I only have that worn-out spare. I wasn't able to replace the tire which blew out last week."

Don worked quickly, realizing the importance of every minute. Within a surprisingly short time, they were on their way again over the hot, dusty, rocky road. "Father," Don prayed, "please keep these tires from blowing." He drove cautiously, trying to miss the countless rocks which threatened to cut a tire or sever the gas or brake lines.

"Two more hours to go," said Don. "This is the worst part of our trip. Not only is the road bad, but there are many robbers in this part of the country."

No sooner had he spoken then he heard a small explosion under the hood. Smoke poured out from everywhere. "Fire!" cried Ruth. "The car's on fire, Don."

The motor coughed and died. Don stepped on the brake to stop the coasting car. Lifting the hood, he saw that the battery had exploded and ignited a fire. Taking a blanket from the car, he quickly extinguished the fire. "I can't believe it, Ruth. I've never seen a battery explode. Now the car won't. . . ." Then it dawned on Don that they were helpless and in the middle of nowhere. The last village was ten miles back, and the strange silence told them they were alone.

"Well, we did our best," said the dejected missionary as he wiped his forehead with a handkerchief. "We will never make it now. I don't know what the authorities will do to us for failing to leave the country on time."

"God won't leave us here, Don. He's brought us this far, and He'll take us the rest of the way too. Listen!" said Ruth, cupping her hand to her ear. "I think I heard a motor."

"You did hear something! I can see it!" shouted Don. "It's a truck, and it's heavily loaded with people."

The truck pulled up and stopped. Its occupants were Arabs. Don shuddered at the thought of being alone with such a group of men. They were noted for their acts of violence in the area. He went to talk with them, expecting them to turn on him any moment. Then they turned to talk among themselves. "Dear Lord," he prayed, "protect us from these men and please help us out of our trouble."

One of the men climbed into the back of the truck and threw out a rope. "Get in your car, Mister," said the leader. "We'll take care of this for you."

In a matter of minutes, the truck was on its way, pulling the disabled car with its precious cargo.

Ruth looked at Don and smiled. "He brought us this far, and He'll take us the rest of the way too."

"Amen," answered Don, nodding his head in agreement.

At last the border gate came into view. Don looked at his watch. "Twenty minutes to go. We're going to make it, Honey," he said with excitement in his voice.

The truck stopped in front of a small thatched tearoom. One of the men jumped off the truck, untied the rope and threw it into the back of the truck. "This is as far as we go, Mister," called the driver. The truck drove off, leaving the helpless vehicle behind.

"We'll have to leave the car and some of our belongings, Ruth," said Don. "Come on, let's go. We must get through this barrier and the next one." Don was staring at the two hundred yards of no-man's-land which separated the two border stations.

Don noticed a man leaving the tearoom, carrying a battery. The sight left Don speechless. He motioned for Ruth to look. The American overtook the man and found out that he was trying to sell the used battery. Don immediately made the purchase and quickly installed the battery.

"Who would ever think a battery would be for sale out here in this wilderness?" said Don as he got back into the car.

"We serve a God of miracles, Don," answered Ruth, patting him on his shoulder.

The border guard lifted the gate, and Don drove into the neighboring country. Beads of perspiration stood out on his face and rolled down his neck. "What a trip that was, Ruth," spoke Don as he stepped from the car, feeling the effects of the tension.

"That's what I call a chain of miracles, Honey," answered Ruth. "By the way, Don, what time is it?"

"Would you believe, three minutes before six o'clock?"

They walked into the small border hotel for a warm meal and a good night's rest.

26

The Life-Giving Medicine

JONAH SHADED HIS EYES from the glare of the setting sun and pointed to the distant village. "There's Chief Mbo's village, Miss Mackey. He sure does ridicule our God. It hurts me to think that he has closed his village to the gospel."

"It hurts me too, Jonah, but God is able to save that old chief. We must continue to pray for him. It is difficult at times to have patience with him. Every time he comes to the dispensary, he interrupts the preaching service."

Jonah bent over, picked up a stick from the road and pointed it toward the village. "They tell me that Chief Mbo has publicly praised the medicine you gave him. But he says that is the only good thing at the mission station."

"We'd better be getting back, Jonah," said Sally as she climbed into the van. "I still have a few patients to see tonight." Sally started the motor and headed the small medical van toward home. She felt that somehow God would break down the barriers that Chief Mbo had erected against her Lord.

"I don't want to hear about your God," bellowed the chief. "All I want from you is your medicine."

"Jonah," said Sally, looking up from the patient she was treating, "look out and see who is making all that noise."

The young medical assistant stepped to the door of the dispensary. "It's the chief from the village of Lepa. He's up to his old tricks again, Miss Mackey."

"Well, tell him to be a little more quiet, Jonah. I have a sick baby in the next room, and I don't want her to be awakened."

Jonah spoke a few words to the chief and then returned to help Sally.

"I think Mark is afraid to say anything to the chief, Miss Mackey," said Jonah as he held the tray of instruments for the nurse. Mark, Sally's other assistant, was responsible for refilling pill bottles for those who came back for more medicine.

"Finish wrapping this ulcer, Jonah. I want to go out and talk to the chief." Sally stepped outside the dispensary and came face to face with the angry chief.

"Chief," she said, "every time you come for medicine, you seem angry and upset with us."

The chief looked at Sally. "Well, I've got to admit, your medicine is good, but your God!" The chief spat on the ground. "I don't want to have anything to do with Him." His words struck like a dagger at Sally's heart.

"Jesus loves you, Chief. He will give you eternal life if you will only call upon Him."

The chief's eyes glared like fire. "Miss, if you keep on with your religious garbage, I'll, I'll. . . ." The infuriated chief shook his fist in Sally's face.

Sally stepped back, stunned by the chief's words.

"I need more sulpha powder, Miss Mackey," Jonah called from the dispensary doorway. Sally kept her supplies in the adjoining storeroom. Jonah thought that would be the safest place for Sally while he and Mark tried to quiet the chief.

Sally, fighting back the tears, unlocked the storeroom door and swung it wide open. She always did that to check for snakes.

Sally went to the shelves of medicine on the far wall. The chief watched her every move. As she knelt to get a box of sulpha powder from the bottom shelf, she prayed, "Lord, please save Chief Mbo. Help him realize his need of Christ."

The chief suddenly threw up his hands. "Look out, Miss!" he called in a loud voice. From out of nowhere appeared a huge, green mamba snake. With its head raised three feet above the ground, it headed into the storeroom toward Sally.

Hearing the chief's call, Sally turned and saw the ten-foot, deadly snake coming toward her. She was petrified. One bite from the poisonous serpent would end her life. The nurse remained motionless in a crouched position. The snake, with its eyes fastened on her, was halfway across the room. Outside, the chief, along with Jonah and Mark, were too shocked to do anything.

"Lord," Sally prayed silently, "help me."

Just then the snake stopped, turned its head and looked to the side of the room. Like a flash, Sally lunged from her crouched position, passing within inches of the deadly monster. Once outside, she turned to see the mamba strike the box of sulpha powder, wrapping its body around it. Sally felt faint. "Thank You, Lord," she breathed. "Thank You for sparing my life."

The chief quickly sprang into action. He grabbed his spear and ran to the door. Taking careful aim, he threw his spear and pinned the squirming mamba to the floor.

"Miss," said Chief Mbo, "that was a very close call."

Sally watched the chief drag the snake from the storehouse. Dropping it on the ground, he looked at the still shaking nurse. "I thought your days were ended when I saw that mamba go for you."

Sally looked at the now friendly face. "Thank you, Chief Mbo, for killing the snake. Thank you, too, for warning me. I know that God used you to save my life."

"I don't know your God," answered Chief Mbo, "but I saw something unusual in that room."

"What was that?" asked Sally.

"That particular snake does not stop at anything. It saw you and was on its way to bite you." The old chief scratched his head and looked puzzled. "Halfway across the room, it stopped for some reason and turned its head to look at something. I didn't see anything except a bare wall, but that snake must have seen something to distract its attention."

Sally smiled. "That was my God, Chief Mbo. He made the snake look away from me."

"Well, like I say, I don't know your God, but I do know now that He exists and that He must be a powerful God."

"He is, Chief," smiled Sally, "and He can be your God too."

The gray-haired chief looked at the ground and took a few steps. Sally's heart ached for him to come to know Christ. Then he turned around. "Would you tell me how I can know your God, Miss?"

At last the nurse began to see some light through the darkness. This was the opportunity for which she and the other missionaries had been praying for a long time. "Yes, I will, Chief Mbo." Her heart beat wildly as she began to tell him about her blessed Savior. It seemed like only minutes before both of them bowed their heads and the chief asked Christ to save him.

The news of Chief Mbo's conversion spread quickly over the mission station as well in the nearby village. Many people had been praying for him.

Before he returned to his village, the chief stopped by the dispensary to thank Sally. "Your other medicine is good, Miss, but it doesn't begin to compare with the medicine which I received this morning. That medicine gave me eternal life." His ugly tribal scars could not mar the peaceful, happy look on his face.

27

Gideon's Prayer

GIDEON SAT AGAINST THE SIDE of his uncle's house watching his friends play soccer. The hot African sun forced him to retreat to the shade of the grass-roof overhang on the small, dried mud-block hut. Every now and then the yelling from the playing field would interrupt his thoughts.

"Oh, how I wish I could get out there and play like the other kids," he thought. Gideon was a strong, healthy young man, but his left foot was at least five times the size of his right foot. Strangely, only the two middle toes and the top part of the foot were oversize. The big toe and two end ones were normal. The foot had begun to grow when Gideon was about seven years old. Now at the age of sixteen he was unable to run and be active like his friends.

"Hey, Gideon!" shouted James, his best friend, "that was a terrific game today. We won that game for you, Gideon. You are our number-one fan." Truer words were never spoken. Not having anything else to do, Gideon watched every game his friends played.

He remembered how he used to play back home in his village. He had played soccer as well as gone hunting and fishing. He had loved hiking in the jungles. But when he was eight years old, a tragedy changed the course of Gideon's life. His parents were out hunting one afternoon and got trapped in a forest fire. Thinking about it made Gideon grimace. He could still hear the screams of his mother and father as they were surrounded by the high, leaping flames.

After the tragic death of his parents, he had gone to live with his Uncle Thomas, a store clerk. Life was different now. His uncle and aunt were Christians. Gideon regularly attended children's classes and church at the Baptist mission. At first, Gideon was scared, but gradually he made friends and became known by the missionaries as well. It was not long before he accepted Christ as his Savior in a class taught by Miss Ryan, a missionary nurse.

As Gideon hobbled back to his uncle's store, one could hear his big foot flapping on the ground. "James," said Gideon as he stopped on the narrow path, "do you remember what we read in Sunday school about Elijah and the ravens?"

James' face lit up as he answered, "I sure do. God made them bring meat to him."

"Do you remember what happened after that, James? Remember God's promise?"

"I can't forget it, Gideon, because Miss Ryan taught the story so well. The Lord helped a widow woman to feed Elijah. God kept putting meal in the barrel and oil in the cruse. He did a miracle."

"That's right!" shouted Gideon. "God performed a miracle. If He could do that for Elijah, He can take away my big foot."

The two young friends bowed their heads right there and prayed that God would somehow make Gideon's foot smaller.

Gideon was so excited he was practically running. Then his enlarged foot kicked a rock in the path. "It's so heavy, I get tired of lifting it," he said, biting his lips because of the pain.

"God is going to answer your prayer, Gideon," his faithful friend assured him.

Sunday morning was always a bright day for Gideon. He loved to go to Sunday school and then listen to Pastor Moses preach God's Word. When the service was over, Miss Ryan tapped Gideon on the shoulder. "Step over here, Gideon," she said; "I want to talk to you." Gideon quickly obeyed.

"Gideon, one of our mission doctors is coming here to Kyabe for several weeks to see some of my patients. Would you like him to look at your foot?"

"Yes, Miss, I would," Gideon answered quickly.

"Well, then," Miss Ryan continued, "come on Tuesday morning to the dispensary. I will see that he examines your foot."

"Thank you, Miss Ryan, thank you," came the happy reply.

Gideon was at the dispensary bright and early even though his uncle's house was an hour's walk from the mission station. "Hello, Gideon," came the pleasant greeting from Miss Ryan. With her was a tall white man with a kind face. "Dr. Hutton, this is Gideon. He came to see you today," said the missionary nurse.

Dr. Hutton shook Gideon's hand. "Hello, Gideon, I'm glad to meet you."

Gideon was getting excited. Was this the day God would answer his prayers? "Please, Lord, let the doctor say he can help me," he prayed as he sat under a shade tree in the dispensary yard. It seemed like hours, but it was only about fifteen minutes until the nurse called him. Unknown to Gideon, Dr. Hutton had had a good look at the foot in passing. "I believe it's a tumor. I think we can help the boy," he told Miss Ryan.

Gideon watched with interest as the doctor examined his foot. His hands went expertly all over the foot from the toes to above the ankle. The doctor turned to the nurse and spoke in English, "Give him preoperative instructions and tell him to return this afternoon. We'll keep him here overnight."

That night Gideon slept in a clean bed in the dispensary. Morning came quickly. It was the day for which he had been praying for so long. Could the doctor actually make his foot smaller? Would he be able to wear shoes on Sunday like his friends? Would he be able to run and jump and play soccer?

Gideon walked into the dispensary operating room. Everything was bright and clean. Gideon was assisted to the operating table. The missionary doctor prayed, asking God to help him as he operated on Gideon. "And Lord, make this operation successful so Gideon can enjoy doing things with his friends."

After the prayer, two African assistants thoroughly washed Gideon's foot and leg. Then a needle was inserted into his back. Soon he began to feel numbness in his foot, his legs and his hips. It was a strange feeling, but Gideon didn't mind at all. In fact, he was wide-awake and could even talk if he wanted to. But he thought it best just to lie quietly and let this man of God do his work.

"Everything is fine, Gideon," the doctor said through the white mask over his nose and mouth. "You now have only three toes left on your left foot; but when the incision heals, you will be as good as new."

"Thank you, Sir. Thank you very much," said Gideon. His

heart swelled with praise to his wonderful Lord.

As he was being carried back to his bed, Gideon couldn't hold back the tears any longer. He tried to hide his face, but the sobs and heavy sighs brought Miss Ryan quickly to his side.

"What's wrong, Gideon? Does it hurt so much?"

"Oh, no, it's nothing like that, Miss Ryan," Gideon answered. "You see, Miss Ryan, ever since I got this big foot I prayed that the Lord would perform a miracle and make it better. Today I saw God answer my prayers."

Tears of joy were falling to the concrete floor—tears from Gideon's eyes and from Miss Ryan's, as she shared Gideon's joy because of this wonderful answer to prayer.

The Power of the Word

"For the word of God is quick, and powerful, and sharper than any twoedged sword, piercing even to the dividing asunder of soul and spirit . . ." (Heb. 4:12).

28

Miracle of River Road

IT WAS THE MIDDLE of the dry season. The hot African sun beat down on the mission compound. Shading his eyes, the elderly deacon called to the missionary doctor who was cleaning the spark plugs on his pickup truck. "Hello, Doctor. Are you getting the truck ready for travel into the bush tomorrow?"

Dr. Sam looked up from under the hood and saw Deacon Luke. He stuck out his hand for the usual handshake. "Yes, Luke. I plan to make a preaching trip tomorrow. Why do you ask?"

Resting his hand on the fender, Luke responded, "Well, Sir, if you don't mind, I would like to go with you. In fact, Pastor Boroto told me just this week that if I had the opportunity to make a trip with you into the bush I should go."

A broad smile spread across Dr. Sam's face. "I think that's great. I'll be looking for you at six o'clock tomorrow morning at my house. And by the way, if you know of any men in the church who would like to go with us, tell them to get in touch with me tonight."

The deacon had an amusing look on his face. "I already have a team of five men to go with us. Your gardener, Samuel, told me you were planning to go on the road this Sunday. I know you like to travel with a truckload of lay preachers; so I already arranged everything with the men."

"That's very thoughtful of you, Luke," said Dr. Sam with a big smile. "The Lord willing, I will see you men tomorrow morning at six."

Dr. Sam laughed as he shared with his wife the conversation

he had had with Luke. "And to think," he said, "that Luke knew all the time that I was going and even had the team ready for the trip."

He walked to the window and gazed into the valley where the mission village was located. The evening fires in front of each hut twinkled like stars. A peaceful feeling ran through his body. "Lord, I thank You for sending us to work among these dear people. Thank You for men like Pastor Boroto and Deacon Luke."

Morning came quickly, and the six men appeared promptly at six o'clock. "Where are we going?" asked Luke.

"I've been praying about that, Luke," said Dr. Sam, "and I believe the Lord would have us go on the river road today." Dr. Sam then led in prayer, asking God's protection and blessing as they traveled and ministered.

Within fifteen minutes, the pickup was on the stony road with ruts two feet deep. When the worst part of the road was finally left behind, the men broke their silence with laughs and excited chatter.

The first village came into view. As the truck entered the outskirts, one of the men tapped on the cab roof. This was the signal for Dr. Sam to stop. One of the men jumped from the truck and headed for the village with his Bible under his arm. The same scene took place at each of the succeeding villages. Finally only Deacon Luke was left in the back of the truck.

"Luke will have a great opportunity today to preach in this next village," thought Dr. Sam. The largest village on the river road was just beginning to come into view. As they entered the village, Dr. Sam expected to hear Luke signal for him to stop. But no signal came. Disappointment gripped Dr. Sam's heart as they passed out of the village. There was only one more village on that road, and he had planned to preach there before returning to pick up the men.

Tap, tap, tap. Luke hit the top of the cab. Dr. Sam slowed to a stop. "Luke, are you sure you want to get out here?"

Luke pointed to four huts almost hidden in the grass. "The Lord told me to go here," he replied. Luke jumped from the truck and headed into the miniature village, waving Dr. Sam to continue on his way.

Fifteen minutes later the missionary doctor was preaching the gospel message to a group of villagers. When the meeting ended, Dr. Sam headed back to pick up his African friends. As he came around a bend, he was surprised to find the road blocked by a crowd of people. Luke was standing in the middle with a big smile on his face.

"What's going on, Luke?" called Dr. Sam.

Luke took a woman by the arm and came over to the driver's side of the truck. "Please, Sir, let me introduce you to Ngossi. She was saved today."

"Well, praise the Lord!" said the missionary. "Now, get in and let's go."

"But, Doctor," said Luke, a bit excited, "Ngossi is the area's witch doctor."

Hearing this, the doctor turned off the motor and stepped from the truck. "Did you say. . . ?"

"That's correct," Luke excitedly interrupted. "This woman is the area's witch doctor. Everyone knows her and is afraid of her. By the way," he went on, "do you remember that big village down the road? That's where she lives."

"What is she doing here?" inquired Dr. Sam.

"That is one of the miracles of her story. Last night she couldn't sleep. Something seemed to say to her, 'Go to the village of Mpoko. Go to the village of Mpoko.' She is used to communicating with Satan, but this was something new to her. In fact, it filled her heart with fear. Early this morning she came to this village. She didn't know why she was coming, and she had no idea what she was going to do when she arrived.

"When she arrived, she went into the little clearing between the huts. Not knowing what else to do, she sat on a log. When the people looked out and saw her, they were afraid to come out to start their morning fires. That was the situation until we came along. I got off here, believing that this was where the Lord wanted me to preach this morning."

When he got off the truck, Luke walked into the village, waving his Bible and calling for everyone to come and hear God's Word. Men, women and children began slipping out of their huts, responding to Luke's call.

"Sit here on this log," he said.

One by one the villagers sat down on the log, being careful not to sit by the woman. Luke opened his Bible and quoted some Scripture. Then he gave a short gospel message, clearly telling of God's love for them and how Jesus Christ died to pay the penalty for their sins. At the close of the message, Luke asked, "How many of you today want to receive Christ as your Savior?"

143

Hardly had the words been spoken when the witch doctor jumped to her feet. She cried, "That's why I'm here. That's why I couldn't sleep. I do ask God to forgive me of my evil ways, and I do accept Christ as my Savior."

Not only did she receive Christ but she pleaded with the villagers to do the same thing.

Luke looked at Dr. Sam. "That's her story, Sir. Now she wants us to go with her to her hut and help her burn her witchcraft materials."

"Praise the Lord!" said the doctor. "Let's get in the truck and go immediately."

As the truck made its way down the jungle trail, the men's strong voices penetrated the jungle. "What can wash away my sin? Nothing but the blood of Jesus. What can make me whole again? Nothing but the blood of Jesus." The witch doctor didn't know the words or tune, but she did her best to join with them as she voiced her praise to her newfound Savior.

As the truck entered the village, hundreds of eyes met this unusual scene. The missionary and three lay preachers were with the area's witch doctor! All kinds of questions came to their minds. Little did they know that a short time before the angels in Heaven rejoiced as a witch doctor woman in the heart of Africa gave her heart to Christ.

29

'Good Words'

"WELL, THAT DOES IT." Dick wiped the perspiration from his brow as he tied the last knot in the rope. "That canvas shouldn't go anywhere."

"Mr. Brown, did you want to carry that extra spare tire with you on this trip?" called Mondo, the African foreman who was responsible to keep the workmen on their job.

"Yes, I did, Mondo," he answered as he headed toward the mission house. "Just tie it on top of the load. It will be all right there."

First-term missionaries Dick and Paula Brown were in their last year of service before returning to the States for their furlough. One of the things Dick wanted to do before he returned was to make another trip up north. He had to travel only about two hundred miles to be on the southern border of the Sahara Desert.

As Dick walked toward the house, his heart beat fast with excitement. "I wish that Paula and the children could go with me," he thought to himself; but he knew it was next to impossible. Peter was just a few months old, and it would be too difficult a trip for such a small baby. Four-year-old Penny enjoyed traveling with her parents, but she understood that she and Mommy had to stay home and take care of little brother while Daddy traveled to tell people about Jesus.

"Has that last bucket of boiled water passed through the filter yet?" Dick asked Paula.

"Yes it has," she answered from the kitchen. "In fact, I put another bucket on to boil. I want to make sure you have plenty of drinking water on this trip." On his last trip Dick ran out of water and had to boil swamp water and make tea with it.

After the evening meal, Dick and Paula went over the checklist together: clothing, food, drinking water, camp cot, bedding, mosquito net, first-aid kit, cooking utensils, tools, kerosene lantern. Everything seemed to check out; but Dick continued to go over the list in his mind.

In the morning Dick heard his faithful African companions waiting for him. Paula had a delicious breakfast on the table. Knowing the road would be long, Dick had a second cup of coffee with his hearty breakfast.

Even though Dick loved to do village work, it was always hard to leave Paula and the children. Penny's words stayed with him, "Bye-bye, Daddy. I love you."

The road was not like an American highway. At times it was just a path, and the truck could barely squeeze through. In the cab with Dick was Mondo, Dick's interpreter for the Arabic-speaking people. Perched on top of the truck's load were Gabo, the cook, and Gombe, the student mechanic. Now and then as they rode along, Dick and Mondo sang hymns with Gabo and Gombe. At noon they stopped to eat. They filled the gas tank by using a plastic hose to siphon the gas from a barrel in the back of the truck. Refreshed after the short stop, they started off again.

By four o'clock that afternoon they encountered heavy sand which slowed them considerably. "Dear Lord, keep us from getting stuck," prayed Dick as he firmly gripped the steering wheel. In thirty minutes they were on harder ground and moving along much faster. Dick was trying to remember when they had seen the last person. Mondo stared out on the plains, trying to catch sight of someone.

A knock on the top of the cab was the signal for Dick to stop. "What is it?" he called as the pickup rolled to a stop.

"Sir," replied Gabo, "three men are over in that field. Shall we call to them?"

"Yes, by all means, Gabo."

Gabo waved to the men to come. Hesitantly they approached. One of the men spoke. With a wide grin on his face, Mondo turned to Dick. "They want to know if they can touch the truck."

"Of course they can," answered Dick.

The men slid their hands along the truck. One of them

spotted the side-view mirror. Dick and his Christian friends were amused as the three men took turns looking in the mirror.

Since it would soon be dark, Dick told Mondo that he would like to tell the men of God's love for them. At Mondo's request, the men snapped to attention in front of Dick. The missionary told them about Christ and what He had done for them. A puzzled look spread on their faces. Dick asked Mondo if they understood what was being said.

"Oh, they understand all right, but they want you to tell them more about Jesus. You see, Sir, they have never heard His name before."

Dick could hardly hold back the tears. What a thrill it was to mention the name of Jesus to men who were hearing it for the first time.

After the gospel message was over, Dick extended an invitation to each of the men to receive Christ. Speaking through Mondo, the man on the left answered first. "Tell your friend that I thank him for coming today and that these words are the best that I have ever heard. As far as believing in Jesus, tell him that the story is too good to believe. Surely the great God of the heavens would not love me enough to send His Son to die for me."

Dick's heart ached as he turned to the man in the center. Sadly, he gave the same answer, "Oh, I believe that Jesus died, but I can't believe that He would die for me in my sin and poverty."

Dick then turned to the third man. He began his answer the same way, but halfway through he looked up at Mondo and smiled. Mondo showed his filed, pointed teeth as he smiled back.

"What did he say, Mondo? What did he say?" asked Dick excitedly.

Mondo held up his hand for Dick to remain silent. "He's not yet through with his answer, Sir," said the faithful African Christian.

Finally the man stopped talking, and Mondo looked at Dick. "His answer is different, Mr. Brown."

"I know it is," said Dick with a big smile on his face, "but what did he say?"

"Well," continued Mondo, "first of all, he said to thank you for coming today. He told me to tell you that these are the best words he has ever heard." Mondo held his fingers as if he was eating food from a bowl. "He took your good words and put them in his mouth and chewed them. He swallowed them, and they became a part of his liver."

"Praise the Lord!" shouted Dick. "What a wonderful start for our trip! Just think, gang, the very first day we have had the joy of talking about Jesus to people who have never heard His blessed name before." Dick spoke some more with the new believer. Everyone shook hands, and they went on their way.

That night at the mission station, Paula lay in bed, praying. ". . . And, dear Lord, please give Dick and the men the opportunity to reach people who have never heard the gospel before." She could not help but believe that God was going to answer her prayer.

30

What Would Jesus Do?

THE WHEELS OF THE BICYCLE came to a halt as they sank deep into the sand. Bill Hall dismounted and picked up the two-wheeler. "I wonder how many more times I have to carry this thing. I'm sure that I've been off it more than on it since I started out this morning."

Bill and Nancy were new missionaries to the Republic of Chad. As he trudged along, accompanied by his African friend, James Boussaba, his thoughts quickly made a rerun of the last several years. Bill had met Nancy at Bible school. It hadn't taken long for them to realize that God had meant them for each other. They shared a definite call to Africa, and they made sure that everything they did pointed in that direction. The steps of preparation seemed to be automatic with them: graduation from Bible school, application to Baptist Mid-Missions, deputation ministry, French language study in Paris, and now their actual participation in the work. The Lord had directed them to the small mission station of Kyabe in the Chad Republic. They worked among the Sara Kaba tribe.

Bill recalled so vividly the day he and Nancy arrived at Kyabe with their little daughter, Sue, to begin their work. They made many wonderful friends that first year. Among them was James Boussaba, a Bible school student who was a constant road companion for Bill on his many bicycle trips to the outlying villages.

"How much farther, James?" asked Bill, as they rounded a bend in the road.

The tall Sara Kaba pointed ahead and answered without looking at Bill: "The village is just over that rise on the trail. If you look to the left of the path, you can see the grass roofs through the trees."

Bill and James mounted their bicycles and pedaled the rest of the way.

"Chief, would you please call your people together for a meeting? We want to tell them the good news of God's love for them," said Bill as he shook hands with the village chief. In minutes a large crowd began to gather. Men and women alike were dressed in bark cloth, animal skins, grass or leaves; the more wealthy were in factory-made cloth.

Before long Bill was once again doing what he had dreamed about doing for so many years. With his open Bible in his hand, he told the people of God's love through His Son, Jesus Christ. What a thrill it was to realize that some were hearing the message for the very first time!

At the close of the message, Bill gave an invitation to accept Christ as Savior. Surprisingly, no one responded.

Bill turned to his African friend to ask the distance to the next village. As he did, he saw a movement beyond the crowd. Taking a second look, he saw an unbelievable sight. Seated under a small tree was an old man. He was covered from the top of his head to the soles of his feet with big, round, open, infected sores. Bill thought to himself, "How can anyone live in such a condition?"

The old African had been cast out of the village to die. No one loved him, and no one cared what happened to him. His eyes were matted shut, and his saliva ran down his body. Hundreds of flies swarmed over him. "I just can't believe it!" said Bill to himself. He found out later that the old man, unable to walk, would drag his body through the village at night. He hoped to come upon some scraps of food or a gourd of water which someone may have put out for the village dogs.

As Bill watched, the old man came closer. Digging his fingers into the ground, he pulled himself along, inch by inch. The people of the village waited to see what this man of God was going to do. Surely he, too, would reject the disease-ridden old man. Bill could not bear to look at him any longer. His human desire was to say good-bye to the villagers and leave; but deep within his heart he didn't have the peace to do so. Being unable to walk or see didn't seem to deter the old man. He was determined to reach the person who brought those wonderful words—words which gave hope to his aching heart.

The village was quiet. Now and then a bird would call from the treetop, but no one seemed to hear. Every eye was riveted on the old man and the young missionary. Bill stood still as though he was glued to the ground. With ten feet separating them, Bill began to smell the rotting flesh of the poor creature crawling toward him. The villagers, not wanting to be contaminated by the smell, moved back a few paces.

After what seemed like an eternity, Bill felt something touch his legs. The indescribable stench and the hundreds of flies told him that the old African was at his feet. In his weakened condition the old man placed his right bony elbow into his left hand and pushed his arm up to reach Bill's hand. The young missionary, who was quite nauseated by now, stood perfectly still, not knowing what to do. He could see the shaking, outstretched arm reaching toward him.

"Help me; oh, help me," pleaded the old man.

Bill immediately thought of his blessed Savior and His sacrificial death at Calvary. His heart stirred within him as he asked himself, "What would Jesus do?" He bowed his head and looked full into the ugly, bloody face. "Oh, God," he cried silently, "help me to see this man as You see him and help me to love him as You love him."

Bill reached down and clasped the skinny, bony hand of the old African. Within minutes the old man accepted Christ as his Savior and became a new creation in Him.

An hour later Bill and James were on the trail again. "That was some experience, James," said Bill as they rode along.

"Yes it was, Sir," answered James with a big smile on his face. "I was praying that God would glue you to that spot and use you to lead that dear old man to Christ. You see, Sir, with the disease so advanced, he can't live more than a few weeks."

As the two friends rode along in silence, the tears began coursing down Bill's face. In his heart he prayed, "Dear Lord, thank You for the privilege of holding the hands of that dear old man today."

31

Tako's Big Day

THE DEATH WAIL OF THE VILLAGERS echoed throughout the forest. Four husky young men walked rapidly down the trail, carrying two hastily made grass baskets. They contained the charred remains of a mother and father. During the annual hunt, they had been trapped in a grass fire. Little did this couple realize when they left their son that morning that, before the day ended, their fellow villagers would bury the remains of their burned bodies. This tragedy was the beginning an unusual life for Tako.

Within two months of the death of Tako's parents, his grandmother, with whom he lived, died of leprosy. Tako had to be placed in the care of his father's oldest brother, a witch doctor who lived twenty miles away.

It was a sad day for Tako when his uncle came for him. Fear gripped his heart as he sat on the back of his uncle's bicycle. Tired and hungry, Tako was afraid to say anything to this man who was a stranger to him. They finally stopped beside a stream. The man gave Tako a dried ear of corn and a handful of peanuts.

It was just beginning to get dark when Tako's uncle pedaled his bicycle into a large village. Tako had never seen so many dogs, goats and chickens. He was happy to see young people his age throughout the village. Some were playing games; others were sitting around the fires with their families. Tako's uncle went to a large hut at the far end of the village. "This must be my new home," thought Tako as his uncle stopped and motioned for him to get off the bicycle. Tako wondered why none of the young people spoke to him. He did not realize the villagers were afraid of his witch doctor uncle. Tako was afraid and homesick.

Tako's uncle motioned Tako into the hut. His bed was a grass mat on the floor. Without realizing that he was talking out loud, Tako mumbled, "I'm hungry." His uncle tossed a dried ear of corn onto the mat. Lying down and half nibbling on the hard, dried ear of corn, Tako fell into a deep sleep.

Tako opened his eyes and looked about the big round room. He saw strange objects, such as bones, roots and broken clay pots. "Now I remember," he thought to himself; "I am with my uncle." His fear and homesickness returned. His uncle came through the open doorway. "Come on, get up. You must work in the garden today." Tako quickly stood to his feet.

Tako ate a chunk of sour bread made from manioc flour and drank a large tin cup of bitter coffee. Even though the coffee did not taste good, Tako drank all of it. He was hungry and ate every bit of bread.

After walking about an hour, Tako and his uncle came out of the dark jungle into a garden. Tako recognized corn, peanuts and sweet potato plants. Pointing to the peanut garden, his uncle said, "That's your job for today. I want you to clean out the weeds."

Tako immediately made his way into the peanut garden. His uncle went into the jungle to clear more land. Tako had never been alone in such a desolate place. As he tried to tear loose the thick weeds, he thought of his mother and father. One tear after another dropped to the ground. "I'm scared," he said to himself, "and I don't have any friends." Tako sat down with his head on his knees and was soon fast asleep.

Tako was startled when something touched his shoulder. Looking up from his sitting position, he saw three strangers. They were smiling. Two of them were Africans, but the third man looked different. His skin was white. Tako was surprised when the white man spoke to him in his language: "What's your name, son?"

Tako, trying to smile, told him his name.

"Where are your mother and father? Surely you are not out here alone."

Tako told them his mother and father had died in a grass fire. He told them of his grandmother's death and why he lived with his uncle.

The three strangers began to talk among themselves. Tako

153

could not hear all they were saying, but he thought he heard the white man say, "We will wait here until his uncle returns."

The white man motioned for Tako to follow him and the other two men. They made their way to the side of the garden and sat under a shade tree. The men opened a basket and pulled out some strange-looking containers. They gave Tako a cup filled with liquid, a sandwich and an orange.

"We are going to pray now and thank God for this food," said the white man. "Bow your head and close your eyes, Tako."

Tako had never heard God spoken of in that way before, and he had never heard anyone thank Him for food. The three strangers bowed their heads and closed their eyes. Tako slowly bowed his head too.

One of the black men, Daniel, quietly said, "Dear Father, we thank You for every provision that You make for us. We thank You for this food. We pray that You will use it to strengthen our bodies to serve You. Thank You, dear Father, that we have the privilege of sharing this food with Tako. We pray that You will use us to help him come to know the Lord Jesus as His Savior. I pray in Jesus' Name, Amen."

One of the men said, "You can open your eyes now and eat your food, Tako." The confused boy lifted his head and once again looked into the three friendly faces.

Even though these men were complete strangers to Tako, something made him love them. He didn't want them to leave him. They talked about a number of things while they were eating, stopping now and then to ask Tako about himself and his uncle.

When they finished, Daniel asked Tako if he had ever heard of Jesus. Tako said that he had not and asked who He was and where He lived. With a smile on his face and that ever-pleasant look, Daniel told Tako the most wonderful story he had ever heard. Daniel had a book which he called God's Word. The men went from village to village, sharing this wonderful story about Jesus with everyone they met.

Tako had never listened so intently to anything. Even before Daniel finished talking, Tako knew that he wanted Jesus to become his Savior.

When he finished the story, Daniel asked Tako if he would like to ask Jesus to come into his heart. Tako almost shouted, "I do! I do! I believe that Jesus loves me and died for me. I want Him to be my Savior."

Tako bowed his head and closed his eyes. He was weeping—not because of fear and homesickness, but because of One named Jesus Who actually died for him. Tako prayed, asking God to save him. When he finished, Tako wanted to throw his arms around the three strangers. Something had happened to him. He felt so good. "I never want to leave these men," he thought. Then sadness struck Tako's heart.

"What's wrong, Tako? Aren't you happy that Jesus is your Savior? Aren't you glad that we came?" asked Stephen. Tako could not hold back the tears. "Oh, yes! I am happy that you came. I am happy for the wonderful true story about Jesus. But my uncle will be coming back to get me, and I must go with him again. I don't want to leave you. Can't I go with you?"

"Don't cry, my son," said the white man softly. "We will wait here with you until your uncle returns."

Hardly had he spoken these words when a call rang out from the garden. "Tako, where are you? Answer me this minute!" Tako's body began to shake with fear.

Stephen called out, "We are over here. We have Tako with us."

Within minutes Tako's uncle appeared. His body was wet with perspiration. "Who are you, and why have you interrupted this boy's work?"

"I am Daniel. This man is missionary Paul, and my fellow tribesman is Stephen. We are traveling through this area to tell everyone we see about the true and living God and His love for mankind."

With his voice filled with anger, Tako's uncle shouted, "I have heard about you and your work. Because of what you tell people, some of my clients refuse to hear me any longer. They refuse to let their children take part in our tribal rites. You are the men who are going around telling people about Jesus!"

Paul spoke quietly, "Yes, you are right. That's exactly what we do. Tell me, Sir, if you died this very moment, where would you spend eternity?"

"Don't give me that white man religion talk," snapped the uncle. "Don't you realize you are speaking to the area witch doctor? It's bad enough that you have turned the heads of many of our people, but don't try it on me. Do you hear?" The man motioned for Tako, "Come with me. I don't want you to hear any more of what these fools have to say."

Tako stepped behind Daniel. The angry look on his uncle's

face frightened Tako. His high-pitched voice echoed through the forest. He shook his fist at the three men. "You leave here at once. We don't want troublemakers like you around here. I never want to hear another word about this one called Jesus." The witch doctor seemed to spit forth each word.

"Why, they aren't even upset with my uncle," thought Tako.

"Sir," said Paul, "we have listened to you; now it is only right that you listen to us before we leave."

Unknown to the missionary and his companions, the witch doctor had been under conviction for many months. One of his few friends became seriously ill and was taken to the mission dispensary. While he was there he heard the gospel and was saved. The man had witnessed to his lifelong friend, the witch doctor, on a number of occasions.

Paul began to tell the witch doctor the same wonderful story Tako had heard shortly before. Surprisingly, Tako's uncle listened to every word that was spoken to him. Now and then he glanced at one of the men.

"Oh, Uncle," Tako pleaded, "please listen to them. Please take Jesus as your Savior. How can you refuse Him when He died for you?" Tako's heart leaped within him as he saw his uncle bow his head. After a moment of silence, he heard his uncle repeating a prayer after missionary Paul.

"I must tell my friend Kono what happened today," said the uncle excitedly. "You see, Kono believed in Jesus at your mission dispensary six months ago. Since he returned home he has been telling me about Christ."

The path back to the village didn't seem as dark and rocky and long to Tako. Missionary Paul told them that if the details could be worked out, he and his wife, along with their four children, would be coming to live in their village. He would build a house of God where he would teach them from God's Word. He would even teach them to sing songs about God's Word.

Tako's uncle urged the men to spend the night with them. "After you help me clean out all of the witchcraft materials, I'm sure there will be plenty of room for all of you."

Tako couldn't help but think what a wonderful day this had been for him. He wished nightfall would never come. Then he thought, "Since my uncle now believes in Jesus as I do, we will be able to start living this new life together. This is even better than the life with my mother and father. I don't understand it, but I know God has made a change in my heart and in my uncle's heart.''

A big smile spread across Tako's face as the five of them entered the village. Already the three men were inviting the village people to come to the uncle's house that evening so they could hear the wonderful story about Jesus.

32

To Tell the Truth

BEN KENT KNELT BESIDE HIS BED as the rays of the early morning sun began to flood the small room. "Dear Father, please help us reach these precious Africans. They are so steeped in superstition." Just the day before several Sara Kaba tribesmen came forward in the morning church service to burn their idols. The Kents could see some progress, but their hearts were heavy for the many who were still bound by the chains of sin. "Lord," Ben prayed, "send just the right men to go hunting with me today."

Shortly after breakfast, Jane Kent stood in the doorway and watched her husband and his little company of hunters make their way to the back of the mission station where they would enter the jungle. She bowed her head and prayed silently, "Father, use Ben to break down that wall of fear and superstition. He has so many wonderful opportunities to speak to them. Use the hunt today for Your glory."

The men walked along in single file, making as little noise as possible. Their eyes were glued on the forest around them. Ben loved these African men. Several of them were new believers. Kebague, the tallest of them all, renamed himself Nicodemus after he was saved. Ben thought of the day Kebague met him on the station driveway and told him that the burden of his sins was too great for him to bear any longer.

"Lord," Ben prayed as he walked along, "some of these men are just babes in Christ. Work through me to strengthen them with Your Word."

Matu, the deacon, stopped abruptly and shot his arm in front of Ben.

"What's wrong?" said Ben, startled.

"Shh! It's a snake, Mr. Kent," said Matu, pointing to a twelve-foot, red, ribbon-like serpent stretched across an opening in the forest before them.

Ben was surprised that he hadn't seen the snake, but that was one of the reasons he always took the Africans with him. They usually saw things in the forest before he did.

"I've never seen a snake like that before, Matu," whispered Ben.

"It's a cobra, Mr. Kent. It's a very poisonous snake and also a rare one. We don't see this kind of snake very often."

The huge cobra lay quietly, seeming not to notice the men standing fifteen feet away. A chill ran up Ben's back. "I'll finish it off right now, men." He lifted his rifle to his shoulder.

"No, Sir," Matu put his hand on the missionary's arm. "Don't waste a bullet on that snake. We can easily kill it with our spears."

Ben lowered the rifle as Matu prepared to throw his spear at the snake. Instead of hurling the spear through the air, Matu sent the spear skimming on top of the ground toward the creature. Ben watched as the spear approached the snake. The jagged two-foot-long fishing spearhead with an eight-foot wood shaft, seemed to slide along the ground. Just before contact, the point hit a pebble. It raised just high enough to pass over the top of the deadly serpent. The long shaft dragged across its back.

The snake coiled, raised its head, spread its hood. The men froze in horror.

"Now what do we do?" asked Ben, keeping his eyes on the cobra.

The angry creature was poised to strike. Any victim would do.

"Why, Mr. Kent," Matu said, "you have the gun. Shoot it."

Ben smiled at Matu's reaction. "Look! Its hood is getting smaller."

One of the men moved, and the snake poised again.

Turning to Nicodemus who was beside him, Ben said, "I want you to step toward the snake. When it spreads its hood, I'll have a good target to shoot at."

"Okay, Mr. Kent. But I'm only going to take one step toward that mean thing," said the tall African. His companions laughed, but it was not said wholly in jest.

Reluctantly, Nicodemus stepped forward. The coiled snake spread its hood. The African stepped back. Ben fired. The snake slumped. Everyone relaxed amid a hubbub of shouts and applause.

"This will be a great story to tell when I return to America," said Ben. "And when I tell it, I want to show this skin."

The puzzled look on the men's faces told Ben that they didn't understand why he would want to show people a snake skin.

Ben continued, "Take Matu's knife, Nicodemus, and skin the snake for me. We'll wait while you do it."

It was as though Ben had struck Nicodemus with his fist. The face of the African grew rigid with fear. Ben wondered what he had said to cause that.

"Mr. Kent," said Nicodemus, "I love you and thank God for you. I have never yet disobeyed you, but the time has come when I must refuse to do what you ask me to do." The silence was so great that Ben could hear Nicodemus breathing. "I can't, Mr. Kent. I can't do it. Please don't ask me again."

Ben could see this was no ordinary fear. He knew Nicodemus was a fearless hunter, a man of courage. The snake was dead. Something more was involved. "There were they in great fear, where no fear was." Ben always thought of that phrase from Psalm 53 when confronted by superstition.

"Why can't you do it, Nicodemus? Surely you can tell me that."

"Well, it is like this, Mr. Kent. This snake is different from any other snake in this area. We don't see many red cobra snakes. Our fathers have warned us never to touch the red cobra. We can spear it, stone it, burn it or kill it in any way, but we are not allowed to touch it."

"What will happen, Nicodemus, if you touch that snake?" asked Ben as he stared at the dead serpent.

"If I touched that snake today, Mr. Kent, it wouldn't kill me. I would return with the rest of you to the village, but I would go back without any arms."

Ben was startled. "What do you mean, Nicodemus, when you say you would go back to the village without any arms?"

"Just exactly that. You see, if I touched that cobra, my arms would drop off right here." Nicodemus placed his hand on his shoulder.

160

Ben listened with a serious look on his face. He knew that Nicodemus believed every word he was saying. And why not? He had been taught this by people he loved and respected. Who would want to put it to the test and face such dire consequences?

"I want to ask you one more question, Nicodemus," said Ben. "If touching this snake will cause your arms to drop off—and you tell me it will—how many of your tribesmen have you seen without arms?"

Nicodemus looked at Ben. "Oh, Mr. Kent," he laughed, "not one Sara Kaba is without arms. You see, Sir, none of us ever touch the red cobra."

Ben stepped toward the dead snake and picked it up in his hands. The Africans were motionless. Ben spoke: "You see, my friends, I am not afraid to touch it. My God will protect me."

"Hand it to me, Mr. Kent," said Matu as he stepped forward from the group. Ben handed the cold serpent to the faithful deacon. Taking it in his hands, Matu turned to the men.

"My dear fellow tribesmen, God has taken the fear of superstition from me. He is stronger than the god of the red cobra or any other gods our people worship in fear."

Kebague looked around at the other men and stepped up beside Matu. "You're right, Matu. Why should I fear when I've accepted Jesus as my Savior?" A big grin was on his face as he reached out and touched the dead snake.

Tears of joy blurred Ben's vision as he reviewed the scene for Jane that evening. "The whole situation was such a direct answer to prayer. Such an opportunity! And Matu . . . his step of faith . . . I could not have asked him to do that. But it was exactly what was needed."

" 'And ye shall know the truth, and the truth shall make you free,' " Jane quoted softly. "That's what they need—the truth."

"That's why we're here," Ben agreed.

33

Poison Bark

"WE DON'T HAVE TIME for you in this village! Take your propaganda somewhere else where people will be fools enough to listen to you!" The tribal-scarred young African looked at Dale and practically spat out the words.

Dale Richards could hardly believe his ears. Never before had any African talked to him like that. In fact, as he spoke to Dale, he deliberately kicked dust at him and spit in his shadow, which was a sign of hate.

"You'd better go, Mr. Richards," an old gray-haired man said quietly. "Come back another day. He may do you harm if you stay."

"Look, Hon," Norma said at the evening meal, "he may have been drunk and didn't know what he was saying. I'm sure you would be welcome back any time."

That night it was difficult for Dale to sleep. And all the next morning the village scene of the day before played over and over again in Dale's mind. "Why would he treat me like that?" he questioned. "I would do almost anything to help these people, and I'm sure they know that."

Dale and Norma were in their second term of service. They spent their first term in the Republic of Chad. Then because of the need for workers in the Central African Empire, they had transferred to that country. With them on the bush station was a veteran missionary nurse, Pat Kern, a Canadian.

Dale was deep in thought when a young man ran toward him. "Mr. Richards!" shouted the approaching African, "please come to our village. Please, please come!"

It must be important for the fellow to be so excited. "What's wrong?" asked Dale.

"Two of our men ate the poison bark, and they are dying."

"Where is your village?" questioned Dale.

"It's the village of Mpoto. You were there yesterday," replied the African.

Dale practically flew into the front seat of the pickup and backed out of the garage.

Hearing the excitement outside, Norma appeared in the office doorway overlooking the drive. "What's wrong, Dale?" she called.

"Two men at Mpoto ate some poison bark. I'm going to bring them here to Pat's dispensary." Dale sped down the drive.

As he came around the last bend in the road, he saw something which he would long remember. The village was jammed with people who seemed crazed. Women were rolling in the dirt and gravel. Some were beating themselves, while others were walking about, wailing the death cry.

"I'm too late," thought Dale as he brought the truck to a stop.

He was met by the village chief. "Hello, Chief," he said, extending his hand for the usual handshake. "Where are the two men who ate the bark?"

"One just vomited up his bark and is over there." The chief pointed to a nearby hut.

"What about the other one?"

"He's in the middle of that group of women," replied the old chief, pointing with his chin to about a hundred women who surrounded the young man. It was almost impossible for Dale to penetrate the wall of women; but finally he made his way to the center of the group.

The young African was lying on his back. His eyes were closed. He was already in a coma. Dale's heart skipped a beat. "Why, he was with the young man who told me to leave yesterday. Where is the other man?" The man in the hut was the one who had ordered him out of the village.

Several women were kneeling over the youth, shouting for him to spit out the bark, but he was unable to hear them. Blood was running out of the corner of his mouth.

"Put him in the truck right now," shouted Dale, surprising himself at the tone of his voice. "I'm taking him to the dispensary."

His command brought an immediate response. Several women picked up the man and carried him to the truck.

"Hurry, Pat! I have a poison case for you. He's dying!" shouted Dale to the missionary nurse.

Pat came running from the house with a glass of liquid. "We have to get this down him," she said, trying to pry open his mouth. "Oh, no! His jaws are locked," she cried, racing back into the house.

Returning with the kitchen stove-lid handle, she quickly broke out two front teeth. "I know this seems cruel," said the nurse, "but his life is in the balance." But as fast as she poured the liquid into his mouth, it came back out.

"Let's roll him over a barrel. That may dislodge the poison in his stomach," she said. The tall African was placed over a barrel and rolled back and forth, but to no avail.

"There's no hope for him, Dale," Pat said with tears in her eyes. "He's dying now."

The limp body heaved a big sigh and stopped breathing. "He's gone, Dale, and no doubt he has passed into a Christless eternity."

Dale stared at the body before him. "One moment here, the next there. What a foolish reason to die," he said. He was referring to the practice of the Banda tribe of eating the poison bark of the Ngounda tree. If anyone was accused of a crime, he would eat the poisonous bark. If he died, he was pronounced guilty. If he lived, he was innocent. "Dear Father, help me to reach these dear people with Your holy Word," prayed Dale. "They are slaves to so many evil practices."

That night Dale and Norma prayed especially for the young man who lived through the poison-bark experience. "Help me to reach him for Christ tomorrow, Father," Dale prayed.

The next morning after breakfast, Dale went to Mpoto. Many mourners were sitting outside the dead man's hut. Many had walked for miles to get there. As was their custom, no water or food was taken from the time they left their village until they arrived at the place of the deceased.

Dale stopped in the center of the village, stepped from the truck and greeted the chief. "Hello, Chief. How are you today?"

"I'm fine, Mr. Richards, but it's a sad day for us here in Mpoto."

The chief studied Dale's face. "Mr. Richards, do you have God's Word that you can give to us right now?" Dale was not expecting this, but he praised the Lord for the opportunity.

"Yes, I do, Chief," he answered as he reached into the truck for his Sango Bible. "Where do you want the people to gather?"

"Well, they seem to be gathered by the hut over there, so why not go there?"

"This is wonderful," prayed Dale. "And to think that just yesterday I was ordered from this village! Thank You, Lord, for the opportunity to preach Your Word."

The young missionary preached loud and clear: "For God so loved the world, that he gave his only begotten Son, that whosoever believeth in him should not perish, but have everlasting life." Dale realized he was giving the gospel to some who had never heard it before. What a thrill to have one's steps so directed by the Lord.

After the brief gospel message, Dale gave the invitation to receive Christ as Savior. His heart leaped within him when he saw a tall young man come from a hut near the truck. "Why, he's the same one who told me he didn't have time for me and that I should take my propaganda somewhere else where people would be foolish enough to believe it," Dale said to himself.

The good-looking African walked straight to Dale and stretched out his hand. Dale shook his hand.

"Thank you, Sir, for coming back." A smile lit the African's face. "First, you came to help Boro and me. Today you returned to comfort us and to give us those good words from Heaven." Everyone sat and stared, listening to every word.

The African continued, "While you spoke today, I received Christ into my heart. I just had to come forward and make my decision known to you and the entire village. Thank you, Sir, for showing us love which is real and comes from your heart. I want that same kind of love to come from my heart."

The pickup seemed to fly down the road on its way back to the mission station.

"Praise the Lord, Honey!" shouted Dale. "He got saved today, and I wouldn't be a bit surprised if we soon get a new student in our pre-Bible school classes here at the station."

Those Precious Jewels

"And they shall be mine ... when I make up my jewels; and I will spare them, as a man spareth his own son that serveth him" (Mal. 3:17).

34

Toby, the Man of Faith

"TOBY!" THE STILL NIGHT AIR carried Bill's voice into the mission village where most of the station workmen lived. He waited, sure that Toby was on his way, running at top speed in total darkness down the path between the mission village and the mission station.

In the meantime Bill returned to the house and took Peter from his mother's arms.

"Pack a bag quickly, Nina, I'll go tonight. Pray that by some miracle the Lord will supply us with men to cross the river. At night the ferry workmen return to their villages in the forest."

Bill heard footsteps on the front porch. "That must be Toby now," he said to Nina, who headed for the kitchen to pack the lunch.

The trouble had started that afternoon. Nina heard Peter cry. She turned from her baking to see what was wrong with her two-year-old son. Utmost in her thoughts were the ever-present dangers of such things as scorpions, centipedes, spiders and snakes.

"What's wrong, Honey?" asked Nina, as she picked him up. She saw that his right eye was swollen shut. Fear gripped her heart as she thought of the many things that could be wrong.

"Bill! Come quickly!"

Bill ran from the garage where he was making furniture. "What's wrong, Nina?"

"I don't know, Bill." A worried look was frozen on her face.

Peter screamed with pain as he reached for his infected eye.

"I'll get a compress. Maybe that will help." Nina ran into the house for a wet cloth. She placed it gently on Peter's eye.

The nearest doctor was a French man in the town of Sarh. The only problem was the river. It had to be crossed by a rickety ferry pushed by long poles. The ferry never ran at night.

Bill looked at Nina. "Even if I drove as fast as I could, I know I couldn't reach the river before the workmen leave. Perhaps the best thing for us to do is to make Peter as comfortable as we can tonight. I'll leave early in the morning and be at the ferry by sunrise."

Bill held Peter and prayed, "Father, we have no idea what is wrong with Peter's eye. Please help us know what to do."

Peter's eye grew worse. Bill and Nina felt helpless as Peter screamed and writhed in pain.

"Bill, we've got to do something. We just can't stand here and see him suffer. His temperature is 103. We've got to get it down."

It was 9:30 P.M. "I'll get some cool water, and we will sponge him," said Bill as he turned toward the kitchen.

"Father," prayed Nina, "help us know what to do. We are so helpless, Lord."

Bill rushed into the room. "I'm going to call Toby. We'll go to Sarh tonight."

Toby was known among the Christians as a man of prayer. Fellow believers came to him with their prayer requests. Many referred to him as "the man who walks with God."

Bill heard the men approach in the darkness, led by faithful Toby.

"Mr. Kent, if you don't mind, Sir, I would like to pray for Peter's eye."

Before Bill could answer, the African bowed his head and began to pray in a positive voice: "Father, I thank You that You are a God of miracles. Peter's eye is no problem to You. I pray, dear Father, that You will restore his eye to normal. The honor and praise will be given to You. Thank You for Your wonderful answer to this request. I pray in the Name of Jesus. Amen."

The young couple stood silently as they listened to the man of faith standing before them. What a thrill it was to see what the power of God can do in the life of one who grew up in pagan darkness, bound by chains of superstition.

Peter stopped crying and laid his head on Bill's shoulder. Toby looked up and smiled at his missionary friends. "Peter's eye is open, dear friends."

Bill looked at his son's eye. "Praise the Lord." His voice cracked, and his eyes filled with tears. He noticed, too, that Peter's body felt cool.

"It's a miracle," breathed Nina.

"Yes, it is, Nina," whispered Bill. "God performed a miracle on our little boy."

"Well, what did you expect?" asked Toby, showing his pointed teeth as he smiled. "Haven't you said many times that we should expect God to answer prayer?"

"I have," Bill agreed; "I have, Toby."

Bill thought to himself, "I may have come to teach, but I continue to learn too."

"He does answer prayer," Bill later told Nina as they stood over the crib where Peter slept in childish abandon. "With God, nothing shall be impossible!" The wonder of it still moved him. He looked at Nina and knew she shared that awe. As one, they slipped to their knees.

On the way back to the village, Toby quietly left his friends and disappeared into the tall grass to spend some time alone with his God.

35

Kossi's Sore Feet

KOSSI MADE HIS WAY into the tiny mud-block church building. He had no desire to hear the missionary lady tell the Bible story, but he was curious. He followed closely behind the boys and girls with whom he had been playing that morning.

He placed his stalk of sugar cane in the corner along with a number of others. Then, shuffling his aching feet on the dirt floor, he made his way to one of the brick benches. Kossi sat down to listen to what the missionary was saying to the group of boys and girls who had gathered that morning for class. Without realizing it, he began picking at his chigger-infested feet while concentrating on what the lady had to say about a boy named Joseph who was put into a well by his brothers.

"I wish those chiggers would stop hurting," thought Kossi, as he dug his feet with a piece of wood he always carried in his pocket for that purpose. The other boys and girls didn't seem to be bothered with chiggers as much as Kossi; but back in the village from which he came there were far more of them than there were in this area. Looking at his infected feet, Kossi thought how easy it was to get the chiggers. All anyone had to do was just play in the village; and, before he would realize it, ten, twenty or even more egg sacs would be growing underneath the skin of his feet. Kossi's feet had hurt him so much that morning it was almost impossible to play games with the other children. He tried to listen carefully to what the missionary lady was saying, but those sacs of chigger eggs seemed to be extra itchy and painful. He couldn't help but scratch and dig and scratch some more. He did manage to break open three of the sacs, leaving large holes in his foot as big as the end of his thumb. He counted twenty-eight more large white sacs underneath the skin of his feet.

The children stood to sing a song. Kossi stood with them and watched as they sang. They seemed to know what they were singing about. The lady then bowed her head and closed her eyes. She prayed that God would speak to the hearts of the children who did not know His Son, the Lord Jesus, as their Savior. Kossi never heard anything like this before, but he had to admit he liked what he heard. Kossi was concerned that he would not go to God's house, which is called Heaven, if he did not receive Jesus as his Savior. Kossi knew he was not ready for God's house.

After the class, the children left the grass-roofed building, picking up their sugar cane stalks as they went. Kossi tried to walk, but his feet hurt him so badly that he sat down again. "You are a new boy in class," said the teacher. "Where do you live, and what is your name?"

Kossi looked at the kind face. He told the lady his name and that his family had recently moved here.

"Let me have a look at those feet," said the kind lady as she stooped down to get a closer look. She gently picked up one of Kossi's dirty and disfigured feet.

"I want you to come to my house and have those feet cared for. You stay right here. I will have my husband come and get you."

Kossi could hardly believe what he was hearing. No one ever paid that much attention to him before—especially to his feet. In a few minutes a pleasant-looking man walked into the church building and greeted Kossi with a big smile. With a twinkle in his eye, he reached down and lifted Kossi into his arms.

"The lady must have told him all about me," thought Kossi. He was quickly whisked out of the building and across the empty lot, followed by a number of curious playmates. Soon Kossi was sitting on a box, and the kind lady was washing his feet in a big basin of soapy water.

"I can never remember their being that clean," said Kossi. The lady looked up at him and smiled. She carefully put medicine into the three holes Kossi had made.

"That's enough for one day," she said. "We'll take care of some of those other sacs tomorrow." She wrapped Kossi's feet in clean white bandages.

While this was going on, the lady's husband found out where Kossi lived. He asked Kossi's parents if they would let Kossi stay in the mission dispensary until his feet were better. Knowing how Kossi suffered, his mother agreed to let him stay at the mission station if his family could bring his food to him.

Kossi could almost see his feet getting better as the missionary lady worked on them every day. In a few days all of the egg sacs were gently removed. In their place the lady put medicine. It burned when she first put it in the holes, but that was nothing compared to the pain Kossi had trying to walk.

On the second day the lady spoke to Kossi about Jesus. "Kossi, would you like me to tell you about Jesus, God's Son, who lives in Heaven?"

Kossi remembered the story she had told about Joseph. Quickly he answered, "Yes, ma'am, I would like you to tell me about Jesus."

The missionary told Kossi about God's love for him. Because of his sin—and the sin of many others like him—Jesus died on the cross, paying the penalty for that sin. Kossi listened carefully to every word. When the lady completed her story, she laid her soft hand on his and said, "Kossi, would you like to have Jesus as your Savior?"

Kossi's response was immediate: "Oh, yes, ma'am, I would like to have Jesus as my Savior."

The lady helped Kossi pray, asking God to forgive him of his sins and asking Jesus to be his Savior.

Every time Kossi's family came to visit him or to bring him food, Kossi would ask the missionaries to talk to his family. He knew in his heart what they should do, but it was difficult for him to say just the right words. Before the week was over, Kossi's brothers and his mother and father had accepted Jesus as their Savior.

At last Kossi was able to walk on his bandaged feet without any pain. So one morning the missionary lady said with a big smile, "Kossi, your feet have healed beautifully. You can go back home today." Then she reached into a bag and pulled out a pair of socks and a pair of shoes. "These are yours, Kossi. Some of God's people in America gave us these for some African boy to wear. I know the Lord had them waiting for you."

Kossi had never worn shoes before. The kind lady helped him by slipping on the socks and then the shoes, tying the laces for him.

Kossi looked at his healed feet and his new shoes. With his eyes filled with tears, he said in a whisper, "Thank You, God, for giving me those sore feet. It was because of them that my family and I have come to know You. Thank You, too, for this wonderful lady and her husband who have been so good to me. Oh, yes, I don't want to forget to thank You for my new socks and shoes. I will use them for You as I walk around, telling others about Jesus."

36

Beoko's Advice Pays Off

DAVE WEST STEPPED from the cab of his pickup truck and headed into the village where the dance was taking place. Just a few steps behind him was his faithful African companion, Beoko.

"Mr. West, we must be very careful what we say or do in this village. This is a religious Yondo dance. They don't want strangers like us to be here."

The missionary turned to Beoko. "Maybe since I'm a white man, they won't say anything. Perhaps I can even get some pictures to show during my next furlough."

Dave could see by the expression on Beoko's face that he disagreed with him.

"Oh, no, you're wrong, Mr. West. In fact, your being a white man could make it more dangerous for you." Beoko paused and then spoke again. "Please don't try to take any pictures. This ceremony is very sacred to them. If we are going to reach them with the gospel, we must understand the spiritual darkness in which they are bound. A little patience and understanding will go a long way."

"You're right, Beoko. I thank the Lord for you and for your help in reaching your people." Dave knew that without the help of his African friend, his ministry could be ineffective among such primitive people.

"Here comes the chief," whispered Beoko.

"Hello, Chief," said Dave, extending his hand for the customary handshake. "We were going by on our way to

Kodro-Ota and saw the crowd of people in your village. I thought we would see if we could be of any help."

"That's right, Chief," added Beoko. "Mr. West always carries medical supplies with him. Many times when we see a group of people, someone may be sick or injured and in need of help."

Beoko's words seemed to please the chief. A big smile spread across his face, showing his filed, pointed teeth.

"Welcome to my village, Mr. West." The chief looked at Beoko and added, "And you, too, fellow tribesman."

The chief led them toward the large crowd of people who surrounded the dancers. The rapid ear-splitting beat of the drums, accompanied by the screaming villagers, made conversation impossible. The chief led Dave and Beoko through the sea of oily, shiny bodies to the first row of spectators. Dave had never seen anything like it. The stories he had heard and the books he had read did not begin to describe the scene before him.

The dancing young people had just returned from their jungle Yondo camp. Dave noticed a number of children taking part in the ceremony. They had tribal scars cut into their foreheads and on the sides of their faces. Some of the girls had holes cut in their lips with short pieces of wood sticking through. A young man danced near Dave. The scars on his back and legs seemed more prominent because of his oiled skin.

Beoko moved to Dave's side so he could speak to him. "Once they have their tribal scars, they are recognized as adults in the tribe."

"But what about those children? They aren't old enough to become adults in the tribe."

"According to tribal custom, they are old enough, Mr. West. Some of those little girls have already been purchased by men in the tribe to be their wives some day."

"I don't understand, Beoko. Do you mean that girls are sold while they are still young children?"

"That's right," replied Beoko. "Parents can sell a girl anytime they wish. A girl who has been sold will stay with her parents until she is old enough to marry; then she must marry the man who bought her while she was still a child."

"But don't girls have anything to say as to who will be their husbands?" questioned Dave.

"A girl has nothing to say about her sale or the man who paid for her."

"Father," Dave prayed silently, "open this village to the preaching of Your Word." He turned to Beoko. "Let's go. I don't want to see any more."

"Well, how did you like it, Mr. West?" asked the chief, stepping from behind a hut.

Dave looked at the smiling chief. "Chief, I believe you are an intelligent and responsible person. This is why you have the place of leadership among your people."

Beoko could tell by the chief's face that he liked what he was hearing.

Dave continued: "I'm sure, Chief, that you wouldn't want to deprive your people of anything good and especially good news about the God I serve. He is able to give you and your people everlasting life."

The chief's smile faded. "Do you mean to say there is news that great that we know nothing about?"

"That's correct, Chief. Your villagers are too excited to listen to me now. Most of them are drunk and cannot think for themselves. I don't think it would be wise to speak to them today."

"You're right," said the chief, nodding his head in agreement. "You speak well, Mr. West. I want you to come back tomorrow and tell my people about this good news of everlasting life that your God can give to them."

Dave extended his hand to the chief. "Well, good-bye, Chief. We'll see you tomorrow."

"Wait, Mr. West! I want to ask you one more thing before you leave." The chief's face was serious as he looked at the missionary. "Would it be possible for you to share that good news with me and then come back tomorrow and tell my people? You see, Mr. West, I am not drunk like the rest of them. I will understand what you say to me."

Beoko prayed silently, "Dear Lord, give Mr. West just the right words to say. Please help us to reach these people with the good news about Jesus."

The three men stepped behind the truck where Dave opened his New Testament. He began to read from the Book of John.

The chief placed his finger on the New Testament. "That's me, Mr. West," he said excitedly. "That's me you're reading about in that Book. I'm that sinner in there."

The missionary explained that these were not his words, but God's words. The chief's heart was under conviction. Within minutes he bowed his head and accepted Christ as his Savior.

Beoko shook the chief's hand. "Now we are truly brothers, Chief. We both belong to the same family—God's family."

A short time later, the chief said good-bye to his newfound friends in Christ. "Good-bye, my true friends. Thank you for sharing with me that good news. I'll have my people ready for you tomorrow."

Dave and Beoko knew that God had given them a foothold for Christ in that primitive area.

37

The Witch Doctor's Curse

"WHAT'S THAT NOISE?" asked Bev.

"Oh, that's the witch doctor," replied Bob. "They tell me that he is putting a curse on our deacon, Matthew. He claims Matthew will die within the next few days."

Even though Bob and Bev Boone had been in Africa only three years, they had become accustomed to the everyday events among the Sara Kaba tribesmen with whom they worked.

"Finish your milk, Honey," Bob said to Sheryl, his four-year-old daughter. "It's time to read God's Word and pray."

After devotions, Bev tucked Sheryl and two-year-old Janet into their beds, securely fastening the mosquito nets underneath the mattresses.

When Bev and Bob were alone in the living room, Bev asked, "Why is he doing this, Bob?"

"I have no idea, Bev. The men told me this morning in our Bible class that Mboro was working witchcraft on Matthew. He fastens a string to a dried gourd with holes in it. It makes a whistling sound as he swings it over his head."

Bev had a puzzled look on her face. "Living among these people, we seem to learn something new every day."

The next morning as Bob was about to go to his workmen's class, he heard a commotion in the backyard. He opened the door and saw Matthew and several workmen. Matthew was holding a thirty-inch snake by the tail.

"What happened, Matthew?" asked Bob.

"This snake bit me, Mr. Boone. I didn't see it when I stepped off my bike. I came down right in the middle of its back. It turned its head around and bit me in the ankle.''

The missionary nurse on the station, Diana Jones, came around the corner of the house with a syringe and vial of antivenin serum. She looked at Bob. "From the description they gave me of the snake, I don't think this serum will counteract this snake's venom.''

The serum was injected, and Matthew was carried to the dispensary.

Already the nearby mission village was meeting for prayer in behalf of Matthew. Bob felt helpless, watching his beloved African friend writhe in pain. In the mission house Bev Boone knelt beside her bed and pleaded to God for Matthew's life.

The morning dragged by as Diana paid close attention to Matthew's condition. Word quickly spread by way of the African grapevine. The general talk in the nearby villages was that Mboro, the witch doctor, had worked the curse of death upon Matthew, the deacon.

By two o'clock that afternoon, the swelling in Matthew's leg had gone above his knee. He didn't seem to be any better. Diana was surprised when Matthew made this unusual request: "Miss Jones, I am not going to die. God is going to spare my life. May I ask some of the men to carry me over to my yard?''

Diana hardly knew what to say. She had done all she could for Matthew. His was the nearest house in the village to the dispensary.

"Well, I guess that's all right, Matthew,'' she smiled. "Since my house is of equal distance to your house and the dispensary, I guess I can come and see you just as well at your place. Just remember one thing. You are a sick man. You are not to walk.''

Matthew looked at the missionary nurse. The Sara Kaba people loved and respected her for her dedicated life and work. "Thank you, Miss Jones. Thank you so very much for allowing me to return home.''

Diana Jones felt in her heart that Matthew had a good reason for his request. Perhaps he knew something.

That night as Bob, Bev and the children sat down for their evening meal, their hearts were heavy for Matthew, a man whom they had grown to love very much. Again Bob prayed, "Dear Lord, please spare Matthew's life. Defeat Satan. Cause what happened today to bring honor and glory to Your name.''

Things were quiet in the Boone household. Bev busied

herself with some necessary mending, and Bob prepared his lesson for the morning Bible class with the workmen. Then a death wail pierced the silent night.

"Did you hear that?" asked Bev as she looked over at Bob. Her face was drained of its color.

"It's the death wail," Bob responded, getting on his feet and moving rapidly toward the door. He grabbed his flashlight.

"Oh, no!" sobbed Bev. "It can't be Matthew!" She buried her face in her hands, shaking her head.

Bob raced out the door to his truck. The wailing became more intense. His heart beat fast. "It's coming from the direction of our mission village," he said to himself. "Lord," he prayed, "help me to accept Your will."

He turned onto the main road and headed the pickup past the dispensary to the mission village. The wailing became louder. "Surely our believers wouldn't wail like that over a death in our mission village," he thought.

He turned into the mission village and shone the headlights on Matthew's house. To his surprise all was quiet. The villagers had already retired for the night. He turned off the headlights and the motor. The wailing continued. One of his workmen, Mando, appeared out of the darkness. "Hello, Mando," said Bob, very much relieved. "Where is the death wail coming from?"

Mando looked toward Mboro's village. "Oh," he said, "that's an old man in Mboro's village. He's been dying for many months now."

What a relief! Bob asked the Lord to forgive him for being so anxious. Since he was there, Bob decided to check on Matthew.

"They're sleeping in their grass-mat enclosure," Mando whispered to Bob as the two of them approached the private enclosure. The entire family lay on grass mats on the ground.

"Matthew, Matthew," called Bob softly.

Matthew stirred, opened his eyes and looked at his missionary friend.

"How are you, Matthew?" Bob asked.

"Oh, I'm fine, Mr. Boone," the sleepy African responded. A big smile spread across Matthew's face. "Now don't you worry about me. I'm not going to die. The Lord still has a job for me."

Bob reached down and patted Matthew on the shoulder. "Good night, Matthew. I'll see you tomorrow."

As he lay in bed waiting for sleep, Bob said to Bev, "Praise the Lord, Honey. Praise the Lord for men of God like Matthew."

38

Amazing Samuel

JOAN HYDE LOOKED down the drive from her kitchen window. "Here comes that old man who was here yesterday, Tom."

"Oh, yes, that's Samuel. He was saved a week ago in the village of Mara. Now he believes God wants him to go to Bible school."

Tom opened the door to leave but then turned to his wife. "I'll talk to him again. He has never gone to school. He can't read or write. I'm certain he would never make it."

"Good morning, Samuel," smiled Tom. "How are you?"

The old man put out his hand for the usual handshake. "I'm fine, Sir. I've come back to ask again if I can go to Bible school." Samuel dropped his head and stared at the ground. "Mr. Hyde, I know I can't read or write. All I'm asking is that you help me get to school. The Lord will help me with my studies." His eyes filled with tears.

"I really don't know what to say to you, Samuel. I do know that you must be able to read and write to go to Bible school."

"Samuel," continued Tom, "why don't you go back to your village and help Pastor Jude? He certainly can use you in the work there."

"I respect you too much to dispute your word, Mr. Hyde. I will go back to my village, but I know in my heart that God wants me in Bible school."

The two shook hands, and the African walked down the driveway.

This was the most unusual case Tom had encountered in his two terms of service in Africa. "Lord," he prayed, "show us what to do regarding Samuel. He is so very sincere, Lord, but he can't even read or write his own name."

As Samuel reached the main road, he, too, was praying. "Father," he said, "I know You want me in Bible school. I ask You now to show Mr. Hyde that You want me in school. Please make me a pastor among my own people." The old man stopped and looked into the blue sky. "I don't know how You are going to work this out for me Father, but I know You are big enough to do it."

Early the next morning, Samuel once again made his way to the mission house.

"I can't believe it," said Joan. "Here comes Samuel again!"

"Now, Mr. Hyde," said the old African, "please try to understand me. I know that God wants to train me to be a pastor. Sir, I beg of you. Please help me go to Bible school."

Tom Hyde was at a loss for words. "All right, Samuel. I will write to the school authorities and tell them about you. Just as soon as I hear from them, I will let you know." He then added, "Don't be disappointed if they don't accept you."

Samuel's face brightened. "Thank you, Mr. Hyde. Now your thinking and the Lord's thinking are the same." The two men laughed as they shook hands.

"I can't believe this," said Tom, holding the letter in his hand. "Sam says to waive the pre-Bible school exam and allow Samuel to come."

"But he can't read or write," Joan said. "How can he do his studies?"

"I don't know, but I'll send word to him right away. School begins in three days, and he'll have to have time to settle." Tom went to the door to call one of the workmen. He had a message of good news for Samuel.

Within an hour the African was at the mission station with his one and only homemade, plywood suitcase.

"Get your baggage ready, Samuel. I want to leave this afternoon for Sibut," called Tom from the front veranda.

"I'm already packed, Mr. Hyde. I have everything in my suitcase," said Samuel. His eyes sparkled with joy.

That afternoon Samuel and Tom left for Sibut. Samuel looked across the front seat of the truck at his missionary friend. "Mr. Hyde, my heart is filled with happiness today. I'm so glad that you are obeying the Lord in doing this for Him."

Tom smiled as he listened to his excited friend express himself. He couldn't help but thank the Lord for the simple childlike faith of Samuel. "I'm glad that I am a part of it all, Samuel," said the missionary.

The next evening Tom sat with Joan on the veranda. "I have made that trip many times, but this was by far the most enjoyable trip. You know, Joan," said Tom, "I have a feeling that Samuel is going to do all right in school."

Joan looked at her husband: "I'm just glad that it is the Lord who orders our stops and starts."

Within weeks the missionary grapevine was buzzing with news about Samuel. "Why, he just sits there and memorizes everything said to him. He can't write his own name, but he sure can quote Scripture," said a missionary who stayed with the Hydes overnight.

Tom and Joan saw a miracle in old Samuel. While the younger students wrote out their notes and later studied them, Samuel just sat quietly and listened. Everyone marveled at his keen mind. The Sango hymn book was just the beginning. He memorized book after book in the Bible. He became a spiritual father, not only to the students but also to the missionaries. Oral examinations were given to him. At the end of four years he graduated at the top of his class.

"Look at him, Tom. I'm so proud of him," said Joan as Samuel sat with the students at the graduation service. "He must be forty years older than any of the rest of his class."

"He still can't write his name," said Tom with a smile, "but he's making progress. All I can say, Joan, is that our Samuel is a miracle of the Lord."

Samuel, too, was thinking of his days in writing class. "Poor Miss Ann," he thought; "she did her best. But when that pencil gets into my fingers, it just loses its way." A smile spread across Samuel's face as he thought of the many who had tried to teach him to read and write.

The next day Samuel returned to Bria with his beloved missionaries. He would soon begin a work among his own people. A crowd of about one hundred gathered around him as he jumped from the truck. The villagers were planning a welcome home party for this one whom they had come to love.

Tom and Joan watched Samuel walk with the local believers down the drive toward the village. A young boy walked beside him, feeling privileged to carry his plywood suitcase. With tears in her eyes, Joan turned to Tom. "Remember that day about four years ago when I told you about the old man coming up the drive?"

Tom smiled. "I sure do remember that day. I know one thing, Joan. We'll never forget the miracle of Samuel."

The missionary couple followed their friends to the village.